Poetry That Will Breach Your Soul

Verse: Collective New Voices

Edited By: Mike O'Connell

First Edition 2015
10 9 8 7 6 5 4 3 2 1

ISBN
13: 978-0692342732
10: 0692342737

Credits
Cover Design: © 2015 Shah Mueen ud Din
Author Frontispieces: © 2014 Valerie Morone All Rights Reserved

Hibernian Publishing LLC
New Jersey

Dedication

This book is dedicated to Mr. Phil Meehan, my freshman English teacher at Hudson Catholic High School. Although a task master, Mr. Meehan had a soft spot for high literature. It was Mr. Meehan who introduced me, and all the other freshmen in his charge, to the whiles of poetry. His bait, Louis Untermeyer's classic, *A Concise Treasury of Great Poems*. Of course, I never realized that I too would have an everlasting appreciation of verse.

Poe, Pound, Keats, Yeats, Shelley(Percy), Milton, Bukowski, Ginsberg and all of the other masters found a place of permanence in my soul.

Table of Contents

Rooted in Love

10 Signs I Shouldn't Have Left

Katherine Kehoe

i don't know how much longer i can fight this
it's closing in on me, it makes it hard to breathe
everywhere i turn, i fall into your eyes
i can't sleep at night without you here with me

i've never had to say i'm sorry before
i've never had to admit i'm wrong
i guess i never cared enough to try until now
i guess no one made a difference until you

i hadn't laughed in a long time until the night we spent together
but then it's always been hard to fight a smile around you
i don't know why i ever thought i'd be better on my own
but then, you've never left me really alone

they tell me everyone deserves a second chance
but what about me? this was my decision, can i take it back?
my mistake stares me in the face everyday
wish i could just back up to when you were mine

you were fighting for us, but somehow i couldn't see it
you told me to stay, told me we could make it better
now i've learned, i never should have doubted you
you've kept your word, you've been there all along

you showed me all these things i've never known
then with a few words, you shook my heart
i've never been so hurt, so confused, so scared
i didn't know what to do, so i took the easy way out

but it wasn't easy, i don't know if anything was ever so hard
now i've had time, i can see what you saw all along
you didn't give up on me, i don't want to give up on you
i want to be there for you, there with you, by your side

you've told me a few stories of people who left you
people you loved, who walked out, who let you down
i don't know if you'll let me, but god knows i've got to try
i'm not going to be another one of them, i want to stay

now you tell me you don't know if we can make it better
but are you only doubting yourself because i did?
i was wrong, i shouldn't have left, and i'm so sorry
you and i had something wonderful and i screwed up

i'm more scared now than ever, i've never had to do this
this is the first i've ever wanted to say these words
but no matter what you say, i need you to know how i feel
so here it is, laid out in front of you - please take me back.

Mr. Sullivan
Katherine Kehoe

Kidneys and heart all fading so slowly
And I'm so sorry, Mr. Sullivan
Those men in white coats left her in your hands
Hanging by almost nothing for God knew how long
Each of your little boys wanted to know why
Really, there was no right answer you could give them
Impossible weight dropped on your shoulders
Never did you stop to take a breath
Every day they needed you to be a soldier.
Knew it was all over as her chest grew still
Even in the face of death, your eyes were dry
Held those little boys who became men too fast
Oh, I'm so sorry, Mr. Sullivan
Everyone knows you did the best you could.
Please remember that it's
Okay
If you
Need to take a moment
To let go.
Please know that those
Little boys
Eagerly wait for
Any kind of sign that could
Show them feeling is not a weakness
And
No one but you can give that
To them.

Anyway
Katherine Kehoe

two words turned my head and you were all i could see
one glance stitched me to you with invisible ties
that existed long before i even knew your name
my heart had known you before, and it reached
kicked down the doors, crashed in and pulled out memories
its pounding was louder than any scream in those halls
i wasn't alone that night, but you caught me anyway.

guilt couldn't stop me from pushing further in
needing to know who you were, why you felt like this
how new arms could hold me as if they'd practiced
and a mind so in tune your tongue could speak my words
we'd had these conversations a hundred times before
and your touch learned how to thrill me long ago
you could see i was squirming, but you stopped us anyway.

torn in places i hadn't known lived inside me
to drop all i knew in favor of this, or to hang on to him,
and leave you in the open to slip through my fingers
after i'd waited twenty-two years to finally meet you again
too hard, shut me down again, i don't deserve you anyway
pushing, fighting, anything to understand what this was
but no matter how i thrashed, you held me anyway.

as months gathered, my pages began to fall out
and as they scattered in the wind, i grasped at shreds -
what i thought would be the final blade crashed down
but you sidestepped so calmly and held out your hand
how could i, having grown into something so cold and stone
strong in the face of something so warm and true? yet every
time i blocked you, here you waited anyway.

even bruised from the riot in my chest, you rose above
and your glow was so bright it crept right inside
all the cracks in my armor i hadn't yet repaired
and from the inside out, my soul recognized yours
piece by piece it melted enough stone to make a door for you
you saw me - the world doesn't, and effortlessly understood;
you know i'm tangled chaos, but you want me anyway.

obstacles grow in our path as the world wakes up -
when we intertwine, i breathe in life and fear nothing
the universe does disappear as our souls expand
in each others' arms we glow like beacons in a storm
map a course for the future; i want you there
and who else can say that about you, baby?
we still have a long way to go, but i love you anyway.

why didn't you tell me you wrote a song about me?
Katherine Kehoe

i did everything i could to let you go
but that anger clung to me for years
bubbling, churning, beneath the surface
i'd laugh whenever anyone mentioned your name
but the word was a piano key through my heart
tearing the fragile muscle that had only just begun to heal
i couldn't understand why they kept bringing you up
didn't they know how badly you shattered me?
and what about you, did you know?
couldn't come to terms – couldn't understand
i thought i knew you, then you knocked over the table
and sent all the cards i'd laid out scattering across the floor
the man i thought i knew would never have done that
or would he?
when you walked through the door again last night,
an apology was written on those perfect lips,
the explanation i'd been searching for - for the past three years
the answers i'd never found held in your open hands.
i'd only just finished rearranging those cards,
and you reached out and brushed half of them to the floor again
but gently this time.
you did what i deemed you incapable of:
came forth with the truth and no walls to be seen
just the boy i'd felt i'd known all along,
vulnerable, nervous, but strong beneath it all.
i have to admit, i didn't know you had it in you
but i didn't know much of anything after the way we crashed
for so long i couldn't be certain of anything.
and to find that out all along,
i meant to you everything that you'd meant to me,
and to hear that through the chaos,
you never stopped caring, i was still your princess

i'd been right, you weren't heartless as they tried to tell me
i felt the last of the anger dissipate
as the tones of your voice reached in to that scar on my heart
and it warmed over once again, began to beat like it used to
when i'd lay my head on your chest and just breathe you in -
it was all i could do
and it's all i'll ever have
if you really want to know the truth,
love is not enough to describe the way my heart kicks for you
the feeling never died, it just quieted in your absence
as much as i'd like to believe it was gone
those chords struck deep inside my chest
and it stirred, slowly at first, but awoke so quickly
to know you feel the same is the most i'd ever dared to imagine
i want you, i'll always want you
i've had to build my life without you in it
this thing again blossoming inside of me
it has to be stomped out before it gets me into trouble again
i believe what you have told me, every word
and that's where the problem clashes against me;
i will never be able to trust myself around you
couldn't you feel it?
it took all i had to wrench my arms from around your shoulders
before my eyes, you transformed again into the prince you always were
my newly healed heart reached out, i wanted to beg you to stay
but i had to let you turn that corner into the night.
thank you for what you finally gave me,
something deeper than i dreamed, full of honesty, pain, fear, and hope
and i got to have you back for just a few minutes,
to feel the laughter, the real thing, that only you had ever sparked, and
to discover that i have never been alone, without you, as i'd thought
then those familiar lips pressed against my cheek,
letting me know the only words you couldn't speak aloud.
don't think it's unrequited; my insides are buzzing with life again
and now i know for sure that this will never fade away

you will never be anything less than the one with the power to switch on
with anyone else, i can just pull the chord and the emotion clicks off
but you're the one with the hand on it, instead of me
the only one in the world who let me touch that chord
maybe you like me to keep guessing
but that's also why i had to leave you last night.
if i gave you control of my heart once again,
how could i be sure you wouldn't push it away this time;
i dare you to show me that i can trust you now
to be everything your words have spun before me
in this moment, i may not be able to give you what i once offered,
but i want you to know, if you ever find yourself wondering,
you were right
there is some kind of love, now you know for sure
you cross my heart.

Zombie Without You

Katherine Kehoe

I walk a barren road full of wasted life
Cut down by choice - They said it was a good idea
And the zombies around me don't attack me anymore
I guess now I'm just like them; they don't know the difference
And sometimes, neither do I
And my eyes are dry - the dead don't cry
So all of this pain is kept locked-up inside
And I miss when songs used to break the morning
It's just as well; the dead don't dance anyway
I guess I still see the beauty, yet it still falls short
Nothing fills my heart anymore; it all leaks out
This giant hole left behind where you should be
While any other holes are so easily filled
This one gapes, and when the breeze brushes by,
The sting is so deep I clutch at my chest
And I fall to my knees and it's all I can do not to howl
And I'm lucky all these autopilot monsters nearby
Have many of the same wounds that made them this way
So when I struggle, they keep walking past
Assuming I am just learning how to deal
How to shut it all down and keep shuffling on
But I haven't shut down at all, my darling
I don't know if I remember how,
Now that you have showed me the way to be so open
And even if I can, I'm not sure I want to
Even though this hurts
More than anything I've ever known
To have found the love of my life
To have found touch, and affection - finally, the truth
And to have walked away
My soul feels like it's dying
Convulsing in anguish, trapped inside me alone

Half of it ripped away so violently
But as long as it's still feeling,
I know it's still alive
And I finally broke and cried today
In the shower where no one can separate water
But I had to stop when Lauren walked in
Pretend - like my heart wasn't collapsing
Most things in life are easier than trying to explain
You and me to all of these zombies

filthy fucking whore

Katherine Kehoe

Your smile was a fish hook, your charisma was the line
Snagged, pulled in, out of the water and I loved how it felt
How I couldn't breathe when you were near me
What it was like outside the ice I was encased in
So long I'd forgotten what it was like to feel at all
And when I broke out of it and began moving again
I followed that line and threw it to the ground
We crashed together, wanting just that feeling
Two rebels taking arms against the status quo
Screaming, fuck labels! we were so high above them
Pleasure, but with freedom, bliss, but independence
Dreaming at night, whether awake or asleep
Intertwining over and over when we were charged
And it carried on and I took away books filled
With words that fearlessly tore from your mouth
A flame that I devoured as our recklessness gathered
My mistake was in believing that I could ever be safe
Resting in bed beside a fire with that much power
The control I'd loved relinquishing knocked me blind
Consumed my insides and pulled them out
And for the first time, we were still, and silence laughed
As my heart finally slowed, I realized
The revolution was over.
The riot had to stop.
You can't bring a baby into a mosh pit.
And that spark you'd fed inside me flared
Not at the world, not at the man, not at society.
But at you
And at me
But mostly at you
How could you let this happen?
What kind of dysfunction could allow you for one moment

To believe that this could come without consequence
There's stupid, and then there's what we did
Which is the definition written by whores and addicts
In one second, you stomped out all those fantasies
And responsibility snaked around my torso
An embrace so tight it snapped pieces off my ribs
And you reached out from your safe distance to hold me as I choked
But I'd rather slap this straightjacket over your shoulders
And let it squeeze your chest and crack your bones
Send them piercing straight through your organs
So all that fire you aim at anyone who gets too close
Could consume you from the inside and leave you ashes
And you could feel this pain, just a little of this pain;
I should not have to bear it alone.

goodbye superman

Katherine Kehoe

i never had the chance to let you know
you were - are - the universe above me
always there when i look up
they say destinies are written in the stars
but it's you that fills me with this sense of purpose
their light sends your strength surging through me
you have a power you don't even realize
no one down here on earth can compare to what you are
we're so small, so insignificant, so nothing
but you lifted me up with you effortlessly,
and you made me realize what i can do
your belief lends me what i need to stand again
now you've vanished somewhere out there
sometimes a star will shimmer, sending me a message
letting me know you're okay, but you have other duties
you can't always be here to save my world
you need to be there to care for your own
i understand
never here on this planet could you have what you needed
in the light of one who shone so brilliantly,
i faltered
i balked
now i've realized how you wanted me to come with you
you never wanted to abandon me
you'd never leave anyone alone
but i let my human fear shackle me to the earth
and i stayed in this pit, while you moved on to the sky
now when i glimpse those flashes of your light,
my pride in what you've done out there cannot be
measured it reaches beyond the boundaries of this
atmosphere
i only hope that you can feel it, and that you might know
if you should ever come this way again

and land on this lonely, half-destroyed world you tried to save
i'll be here, waiting, always looking up
heart brimming with what-ifs and should-haves
but mostly just love, for the being that you are
for the hero who saved me so many times
who will never vanish from my mind,
even when the casket closes over my face
even then, when it's my turn to part from this world,
i'll be looking up.

How Dare You Call Me Weak
Katherine Kehoe

How am I supposed to love you
When my chest feels like it's bleeding?
And you won't let me need you
My pulse leaks out my fingertips
Your labels of strong and fierce
Block my heart when it reaches
You swear I need nothing
But tell me baby, are you afraid?
Do you always keep others at arms' length?
Or am I just special?
You've memorized the combination
And can crack me open any time
But don't forget that when you do,
Pieces fall out onto your body
And little shards of me whisper
"This is it, I'm here, be gentle."
The truth? Gentle is your definition
But your skin is shallow here
And I can't reach underneath
This feeling, heavier than any ghost,
Wants to carry me to new levels
Where love and lust and need collide
And merge to something stronger
And nothing about this is weak
It's relentless and fearless and I
Can brush it with my fingertips
But just for a moment, then it's gone
Shut it fast, slam that door,
Leaving it open is suicide
Because how am I supposed to love you
When my chest feels like it's bleeding?

I Knew What You Were Laughing About All Along
Katherine Kehoe

We left our story on those boards
In a voice that sounded a lot like Elvis
The future looked bright as it stirred behind the glass
Pressed my nose to it like the puppy I was
Amidst the hot smoke I discovered my voice
And the sky could not escape us as we reached out
Our feet claimed the ground even when they shook
But we stepped back, we dropped our arms
My palm still warm from the pulse inside yours
And I never got to grab that future
As the night grew earlier the smoke began to clear
Without it, I couldn't breathe; the air was vacant
But the situation was mutually exclusive
Those nights we walked the streets of Red Bank, we walked in circles
I never handed you my story
But you became so many of the pages
I scrambled to keep my hold, but it wasn't strong enough
And when you looked behind you, the world was waiting
Not our world, the one with suits that choke you
But you went to it, and you found yourself a home again
And she holds you in the way I was never able to
Now the new pages are as empty as our parking lot
To the rest of the world you may choose to be another faceless headstone
But I can still feel your light, smoldering far beneath
You can try to bury it again, but it's not meant to die
No matter how much dirt you kick on it, the embers will remain
And they may not look like much, but I know if I could touch them
They'd strike against mine and ignite so the whole sky burned
Imagine, to feel so much, so alive, all the time
Maybe I wasn't ready for California
But I should have at least pulled us forward.

I'm Not One of Them

Katherine Kehoe

I've never met the women you've loved
But it sounds to me like they were children
Lost in a world full of anger and rage
Wanting only for moments as small as a dime
And that shiny piece was absolutely perfect
Until it hit the ground and flipped to the other side
Those confused girls turned their heads
Both sides so scuffed, almost broken
All they wanted was for someone to notice
The silver that shimmered underneath the grime
 You stood so tall before them,
A beacon of acceptance and understanding
Ever calm, ever patient, a life vest in turmoil
Safety inside arms stronger than the world's hate
Broken as they were, you took your time
Trying to shine all that dirt off their faces
And then they'd flip again, nose over tail
And you'd be left alone with shattered pieces
Of something that was never yours to fix
With memories of how they grew as people
Just for having known you, just for what you'd done
And you could carry this as a trophy of your time
Knowing years hadn't been wasted
You'd touched a heart along the way
You'd been a savior, a protector, you helped her
This is a beautiful purpose to hold true in life
But I've never been a paper doll
I'm not so fragile that I could break if I dropped
It might hurt, but I'll bounce, and I'll land wherever,
I wear my scuffs and bumps proudly
Carrying them as a trophy of my time
And of course I get lost, same as anyone else

But I'll be fine every time, you can trust
I'm not afraid of hard surfaces or dark corners
I'm not a broken side of a coin
I'm both sides, heads and tails, all in one
And no one ever gets to keep me in their pocket
I'll tell you, when I want to run all night,
And dance upon the architecture,
When I want to see you tonight and go for a drive
This road is treacherous, but I like it
This is the challenge I present before you
What do you think, soldier?
Could you lay your armor down?
Could you believe that I'm just as strong as you are?
That I honestly, genuinely, do not need your help?
And if ever I want it, I will simply ask?
Could you stand by, open enough to have my back
But not moving to help because I don't require it?
Could you be still and understand
That I am not the broken heart you're used to saving
I saved myself, and I carry on my own
And I'd love to let you walk beside me
But you need to keep your arms to yourself
If you want to get a glimpse of all my scars
You need to allow that they are strength.
That just because I cry, I am not weak
Just because I hurt, I am not broken
Just because I yell and swear and hit you
Doesn't mean I will leave you
It just means I understand who I am
And I let those crazy emotions rush through me
And when I don't, I'm fighting to do so
I will make mistakes, I will stumble
And if I need your hand, I will reach for it
But don't hold your breath; don't expect
That I, too, am a lost little girl

Looking for you to fix her
I've got all the tools I need to fix myself.

Look at Me Now

Katherine Kehoe

When I drive past this road,
every nerve inside me twists
And I can still feel those nights
when it was your hands at the wheel
Hips glued together with sweat and commands
And you taught me how to forget who I was

I might have spun some wicked webs,
But I was only just a little girl
Still you took my hand and showed me
all the places you wanted me to touch
You told me what I was really thinking,
And I smiled every time it hurt

Your pretty words made me believe
I was so special to you, one of a kind
And I was too weak to make decisions
And I needed this, I needed you
How much of it did you think was true?
How much was a fabricated lyric?

Do you know how long those lies
Were burned in my mind, you fuck?
I grew up thinking I was supposed to say yes
That **no** was a sentence of isolation
I grew up on a stage, performing for many
Connecting with none but your memory

Oh, darling, darling, darling,
Walk a while with me
Watch my steps now, I don't tiptoe
I own this ground beneath me today

I finally learned to know better
Than to let shits like you under my skin

You and I are playback in my mind
A fierce power chord, a crash and a ride
There will never be another
Barely seventeen pieces of trash like you
So when you see me, keep walking
And I hope your regret chokes you
When you wish you had me back

Please tell me when I challenged you to a fight

Katherine Kehoe

Stop!
Listen to yourself
You speak in cannon balls and stone walls
Always armed to the teeth in a bed that should be warm
When I let emotion slip, it's an attack
Shield up, weapons ready, guns hot
Always so quick to fling accusations
I'm a cheater, I'm a liar, I'm a fake, and I'm weak
All these things you swear I'm better than,
You make me into a doll you play with
I'm waist-deep in love and affection
But keep having to fling my arms up
Deflect your attacks and keep my mouth shut:
If I speak up, I stand alone
You remind me of the army behind you;
Why shouldn't this be a warzone?
After all, you chose me,
A girl struggling with a broken heart
Clearly you couldn't have known
You might need to face challenges
All of this sprung up in your face, a surprise attack
As I sit here reaching for you,
And as you tell me I'm worth more than this,
You ask again, suspicious, waiting, poised
Have I done wrong?
Have I broken?
Has my weakness gotten the best of me?
No!
Fuck you!
My weakness is in check and I refuse
To let you, or anyone else, tell me otherwise

You and your overdramatic battle scenes
Can pack up and hike home
If you don't stop this madness, I will retreat
I'm not here to fight you
I'm here to try, the best I know how
As I always do, and if you know me
As well as you've claimed all along
Then you should recognize this shadow
As it stands taller than ever
And walks away from you.

Sex is

Katherine Kehoe

a night on a couch masked by songs of innocence
a whispered dare, hot breath clutching my neck
"You'll never be 'ready', just do it."
swallowed fear churns my stomach inside out
but I hang my head and comply without a sound.

finally grasped in hands that care
this is new to you, too, and we stumble along
"You're so perfect. I love you so much."
so much carries you into me, and it hurts -
so you kiss me 'til it feels better, then you leave.

struggling, please look at me, I'm here
you're half asleep and motionless
"No, I'm not close. Keep going."
not a sound, not a sign, and I crash alone
and you make no move to pick me up.

familiar, commanding, holding me down
teeth and claws disguised as a prince
"I just want to show you I love you."
I do everything you say even when it burns
and you break your words over my back.

rough and scarred, stories painted on arms
but that song tells me you can love anyway
"I just don't have time for a girlfriend right now."
another notch, a plus one to the score
this time is easier; I know I saw it coming.

a new beginning, hope for something more
but a kindness that cannot bridge preferences
"I like skinny girls . . . you're not skinny."
love should not leave bruises under skin
I'm harder to break now, so I limp away.

gazes touching, heating space across a room
a body alone that leaves me in awe
"Tell me what you want to do to me."
only drunken lips can whisper a connection
so I pack my desire again and tear away.

what everyone longs for, 3 am best friends
a gentle trust that transcends time and space
"I really don't know what to do about this girl."
the blow that sends me spinning, was I blind?
those years were lies and I hurt just as long.

a momentary grab for some kind of safe
strange arms never meant to become a lover
"We had fun, right? We always have fun,"
always? it shouldn't have even happened once
now I have no choice but to push away hard.

curiosity, interest, sudden after years apart
different in a way that fights to stay respectful
"Hang on, I want to wait. Oh, fuck it."
never needs much pushing, I just take it
and of course I'm not surprised when you run.

creeping back, a monster beneath my skin
every time I think I'm stronger, you destroy me
"Stop fucking with me. You lead me on."
when standing my ground becomes assault
you don't drive me home anymore, now I walk.

change, a new kind of arms that offer real safety
patience that waits and agrees as I decide
there are few words exchanged in these moments
but I can feel everything I am within your eyes
it's too much, a passing smile is my rope and I'm gone.

a journey across miles far beyond just highway
a match that clicks with all the chips in my heart
"You are everything. I love you, forever."
but dark things crawl inside that you can't fix
so I find a new road alone, and I'm so sorry.

free and wild, where inhibitions fall away
your rebel heart kicks adrenaline into high gear
"I like you. Why do we have to label it?"
independence by choice, touch just for pleasure;
I love the warrior I become through you.

sparks beneath my skin, ignited by your fingers
passion that glows from our pores, yet so careful
"Stay with me. You can do it. Just feel. It's okay."
in your soft moans I find I can still be the tiger at
the same time, your soul fills mine until I burst.

So close, but just out of reach.

Katherine Kehoe

Hush, sweetheart, here I am
Never will the darkness find you
Tucked safely in my arms
A castle I have built around you

These tower walls have grown so cold
I've paced each stone for hours
Maybe darkness cannot touch me here
But I can't reach light either

Go on and cry, baby, I'm right here
I'll hold you 'til it's over
Whatever you need, whenever you fall,
I'll catch you and I'll fix it all

Darling, lover, I can't breathe
Your arms grip me too tightly
Please stop, you're crushing my ribs
Why do I have to fight you?

Why are you trying to run, angel?
You've got all you need right here
You hurt me when you thrash like this
And all I've done is love you

Oh, sweetie, I'm so sorry,
Please don't think me ungrateful
Your heart feels so warm and yet,
Like a stone it sinks my own

How can you say these things to me?
I break and I bend every day for you
I've given up so much for your smile
And you want to throw me away?

No, no, I never wanted this
But what am I supposed to do?
When my bones and lungs are screaming
Under the weight of your love

Go on then, go ahead, doll,
Leave me where I stand alone
I'll cry my pain into the night
For the girl who tore my heart out

Your tears are chains, but I break free
As I open the door and step into the light
It rushes my lungs and I breathe in life
And my tired heart begins to hum

One last glance over my shoulder
Your head in your hands, your body shakes
Something sharp slips through my chest
I close the door and come to kneel beside you

Hush, sweetheart, here I am
Never will the darkness find you
Tucked safely in my arms
A castle we built together

Never have I felt so strange
Pieces of me scattered across stone
The hum inside me focuses anew
Yet again I've bent to stay with you.

The Moment I Decide to Stay

Katherine Kehoe

you know my words aren't as pretty as Brian's
but I hope they reach your heart strings just the same
'cause god knows you've got mine between your fingers
my whole life I wasn't scared of finding love
'cause it didn't exist, a child's bedtime story
then one day you woke me up like newly fallen snow
nose pressed to windows like it's the prettiest thing
nights spent testing just how far this wall could drop
hard floor at my back, and you so soft beside me
fingers daring momentarily glides on skin
one breath, too much life, twisting, pleading, don't stop
but we always pulled away, and I'd feel that ground
and remember this is life, happiness is green paper
this sensation, what it is to feel, not for me
but for the lucky few who dare to believe it's theirs
yet your touch had crept through skin to lie beneath
to spark and spin whenever you reached for me
through the long days of so close, I couldn't break it
no matter how much I kicked and cried and spit
poison can't kill you if the antidote's your own blood
you calmly held my arm and told me, "knock it off.
you're wasting your breath, little girl. I'm not leaving."
months of slower breathing calmed me down until
new doors opened that had been closed to us before
and suddenly a touch was not a sentence
so we ventured closer, and then you bridged the gap
summer and fall rushed so gently from your lips
and inside your chest your heart thrummed a promise
I'd heard it with mine from the start, but now
I could accept it, could step forward, no chains
could have love, and freedom, and trust, together.

all I had to do was open in return
and I took a baby step, scared of the first time
'cause you know I've never done this before
but your spirit is strong and it calls me home
offering dreams that can exist in this world
and your arms never too tight to choke me
but also never loose enough to let me drop
and as you stood back and watched, then I realized
this is what you are: a partner, not a warden
I have whole castles to build myself around
and you stand beside your own and offer new ground
and I can still breathe, until the moment when
I take the step, bold enough to fall head first
and you stop my heart and all my air is gone
as we collide, and the spark becomes a blaze
a shot of gold pumps through every vein
it's beautiful, the moment I decide to stay.

Too Little Too Late
Katherine Kehoe

you don't know how much this ripped me up
those words tore my throat like angry bees on the way out
stung my heart, no, sliced my heart
I never wanted to lose you
you're the only person I could ever see tomorrow with
my safest place, my strongest heart
but right now, all I once felt is locked away
I don't know how to set those feelings loose again
I wish I could, to give you love that you deserve
'cause half of my heart won't do
how could I use your love?
take advantage of it and coast along on it
letting you give more than me every day
no, I don't deserve all you have to give
there's so much inside me I need to strengthen
I'm so sorry that I need to do this alone
I'm so sorry that I can't give you what you should have
I'm sorry that I left you on your own
I'm sorry that I hurt you
you don't know how much this ripped me up

What It Is To Drown
Katherine Kehoe

When did you decide it was okay to close your eyes?
To shut out all the beauty the world has to offer,
And to pretend like you have nothing to give in return.
A blind man can't possibly move forward on his own.

How long did it take for your shell to form?
Once your world went dark, did you stop and stand there?
Waiting, anticipating, as the cold crept up around you.
Eventually, you had to become too numb to feel.

Were you happy with your head under water?
With the world a muffled blur as it passes above you
You would have been safe as long as you didn't breathe.
But even hiding so far down, I couldn't miss that spark.

How far down did you actually disappear?
Now that you're here, you're radiating brilliance
And lighting my world so I can suddenly see.
Was it scary down there, or did you not see that either?

What made you shut yourself off in the first place?
A glow this bright must have been hard to stomp out.
Brought down amongst strangled love and buried dreams.
How cold the world must be to have made you the same.

When are you going to open your eyes all the way?
After standing still so long, it takes practice to walk again.
But you want to try, or you'll just make yourself fall.
The world's been waiting; it needs you to step forth

How long has it been since you looked in a mirror
In the darkness, there was only a warped image of you
Distorted by the numbness you pulled around yourself
It was cruel, it was vicious, and it was wrong.

What's it going to take to make you see what I do?
You were made for much more than just walking.
Your spark was meant to be a fire, meant to burn
You could consume everything in the light of your smile.

All these questions left to hang in silence between us
You let me in, but you're losing yourself in your head again
It's scary to feel when you worked so long not, but tell me,
Wouldn't it be nice to find out what could have been?

Headphones Keep Out the Noise

Nerdgod

Justin Wright

People always call me a nerd.
I'm not a nerd.
I'm a cognitively developed intellectually gifted individual whose mental
development and functioning is of a significantly higher level than the
average human being.
What I mean ...

...some call me a geek, some call me weird
Some say I don't even belong here
Are you made of holmium? Nitrous oxide? No
Then you don't have a reason to be such a ho
Y'all just hating on my success
I don't need people, I got the internet
I'm surprised you haven't been crushed by earth yet
As dense as you are, I'm so hard,
I'm not human, I came here from Mars
What about Star Wars?
My game is perfectly intact
Google? SnapChat? World of Warcraft?
You know I'm down wit dat.
Xbox? PS4? Message Boards? For sure.
And I'm about to mack on this chick
But I can't talk to her in real life just yet
When y'all were just learning how to read
I was doing things y'all still wouldn't believe
Y'all can't get like me
Movies? I get that for free.
I'm so 2023
You're so Times New Roman
And I ain't even boastin'
But the stuff I had last year, you just now downloadin'
Girls hittin' me up on tumblr dot com

Can't wait till your mother log on
No comic books or memorabilia?
Me and my homies ain't feelin' ya
I'm muckin you haters like zombies
Windows Firewall can't even stop me
Cooler than Cool Whip, I am the cool kid,
About to take your school kid
They love me in Japan
Ho's lined up on web cam
All the way to Poland, I'm the man
Even in Australia, bro I hate to tell ya
Just message this girl in Scandinavia
Told her baby, "I'd love to date ya."
Met this girl from Canada
I think her kik is Andrea
You don't have the IQ to do what I do
I'm a genius, you've got a little penis
What I mean is
Thank you for your incredible, irrelevant
Unintelligent, revelation spawned by your hatin'
You're a troll, a failed attempt
And I'm fresher than a breath mint
A pimp, that's fresh to death
And you're a denied request
I'm feelin so fly, stealin' your Wi-Fi
Walk in the club, I got a cool blog
Posted up, I am the Nerdgod

Cutting Deeper
Justin Wright

it's killing me
it's keeping me alive

it's cold
but i feel the warmth

it burns
it hurts
but it's my release

sometimes i sit alone and think
who i am and what is this
if this is a prison
then why do i want to stay here

A Cup of Coffee and 900 mg of Lithium

Justin Wright

Trying to think of a master plan
All I come up with is my dick in my hand
Trying to be a big baller billionaire
All I get is a piece of paper that says life isn't fair

Don't even know the date on the calendar
I feel like the Space Shuttle Challenger
When they tell me to shoot for the stars
They say go hard I just wanna go smart

Every road I take is another dead end
Where I end up drinking myself to death again I
don't even wanna get out of bed or take a shower
Trying not to have a mental breakdown this hour

A cup of coffee and 900 mg of Lithium
A pack of cigarettes and I'm feeling belligerent
People tell me I need to get out more
It's cold outside, people have no souls

I'm feeling like a cat lady hoarder
I want to leave, but I just can't do it
I feel like God is playing a joke on me
Even He's laughing knowing there's no hope for me

It's Just Music

Justin Wright

It's just music
Why you wanna cry about it
It's just music
Why you wanna get so uptight it
It's just music
Trying to tell me what I like
It's just music
Why you always gotta start a fight
It's just music, it's just music, it's just music
Everybody listens to it
It's just music
No artist has the same influence
It's just music
I know everybody got an opinion
It's just music
You need to sit back and just listen

Your band sucks, life sucks, everything that breathes sucks
I think everything sucks – everything about me sucks
I'm so deep and spiritual, you could never be this lyrical
I write poems by the tree; I'm a *%#@in' miracle
'Cause I'm so special, yeah, I'm one of a kind
Everything you do is okay, never as good as mine
My favorite band is, of course, one you never heard of
 I'ma stop listening if anyone gets a word of
I'm so sophisticated, I listen to a band claim I hate it
Your song is cool, but it'd be better if we say I'd made it
We can't be friends, 'cause I always wanna fight
I hate you again, 'cause of something you don't like
Find your own hobby music is my hobby
I found it first, so why you tryin' to copy
You think you're as awesome as me?
How dare you even think you are as awesome as me

It's just music
Why you wanna cry about it
It's just music
Why you get so uptight about it
It's just music
Trying to tell me what I like
It's just music
Why you always gotta start a fight
It's just music, it's just music, it's just music
Everybody listens to it
It's just music
No artist has the same influence
It's just music
I know everybody got an opinion
It's just music
You need to sit back and listen

I'm not trying to brag
But I've thought every thought you have
I'm the realest alive, the truth dude
I'll come to your house and shoot you (probably)
If you say you don't like it
Even if I'm wrong, you are not right, don't fight it
We can write a song but I get to write it
I don't listen to music, I analyze it
There's no point in doing this so don't even try
I'll win every time
I've recited every lie
What I'm gonna say I've already said in my mind
My strategy is I'm gonna talk over you
If you get mad at me then it's over dude
Did you ever think that I have feelings too
No you didn't; you're rude

It's just music
Why you wanna cry about it
It's just music
Why you get so uptight about it
It's just music
Trying to tell me what I like
It's just music
Why you always gotta start a fight
It's just music, It's just music, it's just music
Everybody listens to it
It's just music
No artist has the same influence
It's just music
I know everybody got an opinion
It's just music
You need to sit back and listen

Anybody can spit a verse, anybody can rap
It's just talking in a rhythm; it's simple as that
Everyone's got something they love, something they hate
Everyone claims they real, but they act so fake
Everyone's got an opinion, everyone's got a taste
Couldn't rock mics if you was rhymin on an earthquake
I'm just spittin the truth, at least I'm tryin to
I ain't even gotta try to outshine you
So unconcerned, with all your lies
That's not even a word crosses my mind
Ain't nobody hotter, J Daddy Dollars
If you think you're fly, I'ma fly swatter
Raise this roof like I'm your father
But I am your father, so call me daddy
Said she was tired of the small talk
So I rap about my dick

Held Under Glass
Justin Wright

Beautiful things came from the dark
Next time you're feeling down take a walk in the park
You'll look at life with a complete new start
Nothing is greater than the strength of your heart
I wanna feel alive, I want peace of mind, I
I wanna see the beauty that's kept inside, life
Can be paradise it just depends
How many times you're willing to get back up again
What you're searching for is already within
It's true, you'll get through, just believe in you
You can't change things you didn't do
I guess that means I'm just a sucker for hope
I don't give up easy, never, nope
Even in my nightmares I'm somewhere dreaming
I believe nothing can ever stop you from succeeding
If nothing stops you from believing, find the meaning

And I know just how you feel
The pain is just too real
You feel like you've lost your way
But everything will be okay

Beautiful things came from the dark
Your searching for some way to find that spark
Trying to pick up the pieces but you're fallen apart
Feels like someone just took a knife to your heart
Your head's filled with doubt,
thinking what now?
You wanna figure it out,
you just don't know how
You wanna get back up but you're hurt from the fall
But before you can walk you gotta learn to crawl

If you fall, don't be ashamed, you'll get up again
It's okay, you'll find a way, to rise above the flames
When you're at the bottom there's only one way to go
Let depression know, I can't be your host,
Grab life by the throat, and Ju-Jitsu that bitch
Let it know you ain't having this shit
And it ain't handed to you, you gotta take action
But life's easy when you got passion, make it happen

No one can do it for you (Forget the past!)
It's up to you to pull through (Don't look back!)
You'll find a way to find your way
Everything will be okay

Never Apologize

Justin Wright

I'll never say I'm sorry for being me
Never apologize for something I mean
You can't teach a dog to run free
You can't make someone see
What they don't wanna believe

I know I'm crazy, I don't care
Everything's alright as long as you're here
You don't have to lie to me
Will be what I will be

I can make you smile and make you laugh
I act like a child but I'm okay with that
As long as you'll let me stay here with you
I can change but only if I want to

They wanna tear us down
So I guess I'm just a clown
I'm not normal but I don't mind
I'm okay with that - it's alright

Eraseless
Justin Wright

Something's wrong, you can't put it into words
So you make up things not caring who it hurts
So much pain from the feelings that you can't explain
Are you sick in the brain, why do you feel this way?
What's going on with you, you're so confused
You don't have a clue, so what's the use?
You're looking for a way in the wrong places
The bed that you made is eraseless

Eraseless
Eraseless
So Eraseless

There's a place so dark everything beautiful dies
Everything here is dead inside
A place so dark everything beautiful dies

This hole in your heart is a void you can't fill
So you replace it with something that ain't real
You've changed so much, you don't even know how to feel
How can you expect for these old wounds to heal?
So distant, what you are trying to be?
No one listens, they don't know what to believe
You're persistent, but they're distant as hell
You'll try anything to get recognition yourself
Another lie, story - Another cry, ignored plead
Another I before Me - Another why can't you see
Can't get up, from this rut, it's no luck
You're stuck, you throw up, you scratch and cut
But no matter what it never becomes enough
Someone to talk to, not one who can talk to you
You're trapped inside every little thing you do

All the life lines that you've wasted
Are nowhere to be found amongst the nameless

The nameless
The nameless
So nameless

And you try (try) to escape the pain
No matter what you do, you stay the same
Why (why), why do you feel this way
No matter what you do you're still the same

Seeking attention is a sad game you play
No one listens to a damn thing you say
It brings you down when friends are not around
They laugh, is it so bad, that they have doubts
What's worse is you need help, you're hurting yourself
Do you really think no one else feels the hell you felt?
Life's hard everyone has scars even if they don't show it
You'll find what you're looking for and not even know it
You're looking for a way out in all the wrong places
It's nowhere to be found amongst the nameless

You're wanting something so bad
And once you get it, you'll wish you never had
Where it's at there's no turning back
You're swimming in dirt with the sharks
Where everything beautiful turns to the dark
There is no hope just suffering and doubt
Everyone that makes it here never comes out
You can go, but never leave, so cold and empty
Everything you once loved is now missing
A prison, non-existence and confusion
An empty shell living inside of a human
Some win but everyone does the losing

Alone can be the worst pain there is
You're nothing amongst the faceless

The faceless
The faceless
Trapped in the fakeness

Sexual Grandpa
Justin Wright

Diss me and you're about to start a riot
I'm not Tsarnaeva, I'm not going out quiet
Shout out my name, you're clearly not thinking
You're career's over as soon as my pen starts leaking
Have you heard the tracks I been making lately
You'll just look like a hater if you say you hate me
If hip hop's dead then I'm about to save it
And I ain't gotta pay DJ's to play it
Says something about you if you hate it
My style's so new even if you duplicate it
I'll change it, and come up with something fresher
So much dope coming out the lab call me Uncle Fester
You want me to come at you in a song
You'd rather have Tyson come at your jaw
It's not, f ya'll, but I don't mess with ya'll
Make the monopoly money dog
You're looking, but you're not seeing
I know you think you're bling blingin'
Hate to say it but your ship's sinkin'
I'm back in the game Grim Reapin'
We know that you're just lying to 'em
You'll have to copy what I am doin'
To stay relevant in this game
It's all about the change
Oh you thought you could get rid of me
Let it go, so sick of your negativity
This dumb flow is so much smarter
I'm sicker than a sexual grandpa
So make that monopoly money ya'll
I let it all hang out, I put my dick on the paper

Your style's about as fresh as CD players
I'm not fake, that's why my plan's working
i'm going after you snakes like Steve Irwin

Tourette On Crack
Justin Wright

Food and sleep take away my pain
The only two things that keep my sane
I either gotta get it right or take a bullet to the brain
I don't wanna be negative or complain
But so many things are dragging me down
It's like I'm waiting for something that never comes around
And I know I ain't gonna find it just dreaming
But I can't figure out if I'm alive or just breathing
Don't wanna die but I don't wanna live
Eventually you would think something's got to give
I guess I'll figure it out or I won't
You either swim or you don't
I think this world is a mess and people think I'm wrong
So I guess I'll just let it out on another song
Everybody's gotta play their own hands
But I'm tired of being dealt the ones no understands
I don't need your advice or your heart to heart talk
You might be able to put yourself in my shoes but I dare you to walk
Some people will burn you over money
Others don't even need a reason trust me
Can't find a friend that don't wanna play you
Can't talk about your problems without feeling mentally raped too
Thankful I got tumblr, nothing is funnier,
If not I'd be slicing my jugular
If I'm not being real with myself then I'm not living right
And I wouldn't be being true if I told you everything's alright
I might sound like a Tourette on crack
Or I might sound like I'm saying the facts
I don't wanna die, but let's just say
If a car was coming toward me I wouldn't jump out the way

Headphones

Justin Wright

Sometimes I feel like I don't know how to feel
Like when Trayvon Martin got killed
Two sides of the story and I wasn't there
So who am I to say the verdict wasn't fair?
People judge what they don't know, until it happens to them
If you were under the microscope, what would happen then?
I turn on the tv and it's a story of the same kid
They blame his parents for the way they raised him
So they send him to another doctor's office
So they can figure out what his problem is
Instead he turns to cutting and pills
So I write this when a beat gives me the chills
'Cause it's the only way I know how to cope
It's my release, for me it's hope
And I wish I could fight for those who can't fight for themselves
You just say they're weak when they cry for help

I turn on the news, all they do is run their mouth
Telling people how to live like they got it figured out
But they ain't got a clue, they're just adding fuel
To the fire the one Billy Joel tried to tell you!
You never see Nancy Grace on sixty minutes
Ask Alanis, it's a little too ironic isn't it?
What about the damage the news media causes us?
We're supposed to accept that isn't where the problem is huh?
No matter how hard you try, people will think for themselves
I bet if you looked closer you'd see Dr. Phil needs help
What kind of person thinks everyone else is wrong?
So don't act like you know us all
Why is Kesha's song the number one on the radio
But if you go on YouTube it's barely getting played though?

It makes me wonder what I could do with money
Could I buy fame and pay people to love me?

Through these headphones
I found a way to escape
An outlet that could replace my hate

Through my words
I could paint my pain
A picture that could erase my shame

Strange
Justin Wright

This demon won't disappear
Inside you, it's everything you fear
Don't wanna stay but you belong here
Because different is always just weird

A joke behind every smile
A monster behind every child
Everything you do is so good
But no matter what, still no good

You want the feelings to stop
But you become something you're not
There's no in-between
You're the I without the M or the E

Your nightmares are your dreams
Where some look but never actually see
You wanna fit but not exist
And shift among the midst

You are yourself and no one else
And they can't help you, they're nothing special
They can't see because they're blind
They don't understand - they have no mind

They're fake; they only know fear
They hate; they want to be cheered
They can't feel; they're ashamed
They're not real, they'll only fade away

Number one is number strange
Number two is everything the same

So Sick I Need Dr Oz

Justin Wright

I'm 26 still acting like a kid
Threatening to kill myself
And you still don't give a shit

I'm such a drama queen
I'm seeking attention
I think you're so mean

Am I dead or is this depression
I need a lot of answers
That's why I ask questions

Am I dying or is it another symptom
I don't expect you to care
I didn't think you would listen

One day I get better
The next I'm worse
Never know if I'm writing my suicide letter

How can I be like you
And make up lies
When we know the truth

So worried about your ego
You right or wrong me
When we know

Are some things better unsaid
Or is the truth too much to admit
I guess I made my bed

I feel like I'm still four years old
Trying to make you understand
So I won't say I told you so

Not everyone's looking for sympathy
I mean what would be the use
When you can't do nothing for me

People aren't allowed to be people anymore
Everyone thinks they got it worse
Blinded by pride they choose to ignore

Sadness got me feeling like I'm on life support
Have I said too much
Or did my honesty strike a chord

All I know is that we're all human
Instead of trying to work things out
You'd rather make excuses

Some win but everyone is losing
You've got all the answers
Lost in your own confusion

Tell me when was the last time
You saw someone stand for someone
When no one stood by my their side

2 Stories

Justin Wright

He said I don't have no one, dad never cared
My mom stares at the wall, she's never there
Loaded on prescriptions can't figure out her sickness
She can't see that her addiction is her biggest symptom
I try to tell her she won't listen, her head is a prison
Laying wasted takes its toll, I try to tell her she can't be told
Medication's got such a hold, thinks she's got it in control
On her, I wonder, what will happen, I keep praying and askin
Too many things I can't stand, wanna get away but I can't
Afraid I'll find her on the floor with her head in her hands
What makes it worse is her friends have the same habit
So she thinks that everybody in this world's an addict
She can't see they're as messed up as she is
She doesn't even leave the house to see her kids
Dresser's full of empty bottles, in and out of hospitals
What's gonna happen tomorrow
It's such a problem, she can't fix her own problems
I don't know what to do, I've run outta options

2

She said I'm embarrassed, I'm ashamed
I feel like it's my fault that I feel this way
I try to explain but I don't know what to say
I wanna escape but I'm afraid, to cross that line
Everything's grey, nothing's black and white
I just lie, about the bruises on my eyes
I tell you I'm fine, but it happens all the time -
I'm not seeking attention, it's just offensive
When she says "don't tell" to anyone who listens
This depressing image, a secret I've kept hidden
No one can know, he lost control, I forgive him
I sink my nails in his skin, but I always give in

He's too strong and he'll just hit me again
I keep my eyes shut, when he comes home drunk
Hoping he won't notice, he won't wake me up
My neighbor sees but he won't intervene
Maybe he's just as scared as me

What if it was you,
That had to step in someone else's shoes?
Would you still pass judgment like you do?

Black, Red, White, and Blue

if i die

Stephanie Lynn Maxwell

and you find me sailing in the skies on a cloud of forever
and if you find me on a maple leaf flowing in the fall wind
and if you find me along the tides of the Atlantic clinging to the rocks
and if you find me dancing with the man on the moon
and if you find me riding the glowing rays of sunrise
and if you find me as the daisy growing in your rose garden
and if you find me on the tip of your nose as spring tickles your spirit
and if you find me crossing your mind when feel that sudden chill
that makes you shiver

find comfort
and know that it indeed is
me

Stay Awake

Stephanie Lynn Maxwell

I lie with my eyes wide open – I need to see the evil of my dreams
that lurks around the corner
to rapture any ounce of light left from the day that left me wounded
I watch the moonlight as it makes its way through the trees
                                    creating shadows of claws
of death and gnashing, gnarly teeth

 I once fell asleep to the sound of night rain and was awoken to the crash of
                          evil and lightening flashed the devil's face
and then I was in pain

        I don't dare close my eyes at night for fear I will not see the disgusting
                                    demons that await me
in my sleep
when I had awakened it was not a dream
and then I was in pain

Maybe I shall never sleep again

One Cannot Be Trusted

Stephanie Lynn Maxwell

your words may be woven around my heart like a quilt
and the meaning behind black and white may move mountains
But you're still a man

your power over is enticing
and tempting
and the way you can maneuver my emotions is nothing short of amazing
But you're still a man

your ways attract me like a bee to pollen and it seems I cannot get enough
and it seems I have grown accustomed
and it seems I cannot go a day without you
But you're still a man

and whilst it is as if you can be trusted
as if your words weren't true
and although you never made the promise
you still place the knife where it's due
You're still a man

with my jealous heart
I shall try to forget
though I will always remember
though I will always know
My words had a slither of dishonesty too

so it is in return
I put the knife into you

Photograph
Stephanie Lynn Maxwell

I used to look at your smile and laugh
but now it makes me cry
you're no longer amongst us in the physical world
you are only the memories I desperately cling to
the pictures I kiss every day
you are a spirit in the sky

My friend, the sweetest I had ever known
he would give you the shirt off his back
if you needed it - you know
even if he didn't have any to give, he would dig deep for a stranger
he knew and understood the struggle
he knew the love of the word
he knew the love of a child
he had the best laugh you had ever heard

I wish I could feel your hugs again
they were the best
I could be hurt, sad, lonely; just the sight of you lifted Satan off my
chest

You were too good to be here
I guess that's why God took you so soon

You were better fit for His kingdom
and if I ever get to see you again,
then I hope I am too.

The Cave
Stephanie Lynn Maxwell

a wave of sadness over takes my body
as I vomit self-esteem
it never belonged within me anyway
that was never me
under the boulder of self-pity inside a cave of broken dreams
the little girl is still hiding from the monsters
and holding on to what used to be
with ribbons in her hair and shoes that never fit
the awkwardness of being different was all they'd ever see
she's crying
i'm crying
the storm is never over
the lightening flash is frightening
we're losing air in the thunder
now we can't breathe
who is coming to save us
who is coming to save me
beneath this boulder of sadness
in a cave of broken dreams

Dear America,
Stephanie Lynn Maxwell

Thank you

For this place you call the land of the free;
a land full of debt, poverty and incurable disease

A natural disaster can wipe a city completely off the map,
but financial assistance is rejected because another country needed it

Blow up a nation to build a government that's non-existent,
while you've lost all interest of your own resulting in a crumbling system

You ramp up the cost of living and lower the level of pay – all those jobs
that only require simple skills you send overseas to give away

Working hard and growing old was once the American Dream; we still
pay our last pennies into that same bank – money we will never see

Illegal immigration a topic of social exception – fool the people into
thinking – no economic crisis with your emotional campaign deception

Require expensive, extensive college degrees for only common sense
then pay minimum wage so that people are forever in debt

Control everything we do, yet still give us freedom of speech
So that we can only talk of our dreams and never practice what we preach

Commit a murder in Illinois and you're behind bars forever on your knees
Commit that same crime in Florida and you're guaranteed to be free

Two of the same exact persons in dire need of the same heart,
One has enough money in his pockets giving him a head start,
While the poor man is sentenced to death for not doing his part

America, what happened?
This is no longer your land
and it's no longer my land
it's simply crumbling cliffs of
old foundations
sifting into sand

Red
White
Blue

What do these colors mean to you?

nightmares
Stephanie Lynn Maxwell

The safest place is supposed to be my dreams
but it seems that when the devil
tends to attack me most
comforting warmth and sleepy slumber
disturbed by horrific fear
caught beneath my throat
expelled in blood-curdling
screams

be anything but real

Stephanie Lynn Maxwell

Please,
will you make love to me so bad it
hurts?
So that I cannot tell the pain in my heart is worse.

Please,
will you leave marks of agony
on my skin?
So that I cannot sense the suffering.

Please,
will you say how much you love me
even if for one night?
So that I can be lost in the moment
and the moment be right.

#TheStruggle
Stephanie Lynn Maxwell

my mother has blue eyes
but I'm still a nigger
my mother has blonde hair
but I'm still a nigger
my daddy is black as night
but I'm still a cracker
my daddy has kinky curls
but I'm still a cracker

I call this hash tag the struggle
because to be biracial is nothing
more
because to be biracial is nothing
less
than a struggle
to find who I am
to find who I should be
to find who I'm supposed to be

i really wish they were the same person
i really wish you understood hash tag the struggle
but you don't
but you won't

so stop telling me about my
good hair
and stop telling about my high
yellow skin
and stop telling me my parents have the fever
and stop staring at me when I
walk in

and stop trying to guess which parent is black
and stop trying to guess which parent is Spanish

No

I'm not Spanish

No

I don't speak Spanish

No

You CANNOT touch my hair

Yes, my nose is in the air
Of course I think I'm the shit
 I live my life trying to be better than women who are dark skinned
. . . with something
I was born with
. . . out of my control
Of course I try to flaunt my plush lips around white girls who get Botox
who then become the have-nots because I've stolen all the brothas hearts
from the city and the boondocks

See you don't even know me
but you think these are my goals

see, I call this hash tag the struggle because nobody understands
the trouble in being whole
when you're given two halves
that don't match to patch up one soul
and you're born into a fucked up mess still expected to know

and they tell you to ignore them all
be yourself
race should not define you
but I can't even fill out two fucking boxes on a standardized test
because you are only allowed to check ONE to describe you

hash tag
TheStruggle

aspects of ME.
Stephanie Lynn Maxwell

If I told you the dark frightens me
and the winds move me
and the waters soothe me
and the rain aroused me
and the sun astounds me
Would you believe?

If I told you hurt makes my work
twice as hard than the next
that each insecurity inhaled with each breath
is even harder to exhale until there is not much of me left
Would you believe?

If I told you the cool touch of a blade
(the silliest decision ever made)
provides an outlet of aggressive and inner decay within a thin line
of addiction and seeming okay
Would you believe?

If I told you I solemnly swear to the pit of my existence to be that I can
tell the truth as it lies
knead the world in my hands so that success may just happen to rise
while in hopes of drying old tears from my eyes
Would you believe?

so i know this poet
Stephanie Lynn Maxwell

and like a delicate petal of rose drifting upon my cheek
he sends the softest kisses within his words
making me blush with songs unheard – i sense the truth within
i've become careless
i've given in
sharing secrets of secrets and lines of phrases
preaching poems of love and lusty praises
we have found a hiding place that only we understand
and we can carry on into the lightening of darkness; into the sun;
into the sand; into the ocean; into the sky deep into our . . .

mind

the imagination is truly a beautiful place and it is that place i found
parts of me i had never known
it is that place there are parts of me that i have never shown
and i was able to share all my nakedness in all its glory
and i need not undress
for he did that for me
and just like that with the simple touch of his being
and the tongue in his words
and his ability to envision the picture without seeing
he tied me up with his . . .

mind

a connection made in black and white
binds the strings of wrong and right
early morning and late at night
friendship lust and morals fight

how do i feel entitlement to what isn't mine
what doesn't belong to me
what doesn't exist?
the lovely language of a lovely poet is enticingly hard to resist
its begins in the . . .

mind

Fifth Sense

Stephanie Lynn Maxwell

Close your eyes and let me show you how it's real
It's not by sight that leads us
It's the flesh upon flesh and the rhythm of that pound in your chest
to your very core you'll feel
Hold my hips and let me plant the sweetest kiss
I can dry your tears
I can heal your hurt
I promise you this
And when I take you for granted know that I never mean it
know that where I come from is a deep place of truth
I am overflowing from the idea of you
Let me be your all and everything in between
Let me be your world
your downfall
Let me be your queen

In sweet harmony
In agonizing demise
Close them tight and hold me forever
Don't ever open your eyes

perhaps a wolf in sheep's clothing

Stephanie Lynn Maxwell

last night I dreamt of lying in your arms under a moonlit stricken sky
and you whispering things I could not understand; they made me giggle
so I assumed they were good things

good things

and you devoured me whole into your world and showed me the stars
and what it feels to fly on cloud number nine
not once did you ever let me go

let me go

and when we were done swimming in passion in the heat of the night
you sent me straight to hell and
all the good was gone

good was gone

who are you?

Why Me
Stephanie Lynn Maxwell

Why not the asshole who just robbed the old man at the corner store
Why not the lady who crack induced her own abortion – she didn't want a
baby no more
Why not the gang banger who killed a man just for his name
Why not the dishonest greedy businessman always begging for change
Why not the creep at church that gets away with touching little kids
Why not the guilty pastor that knew about it yet acted like he never did
Why not the ungrateful mother that enjoys bullying her seed
Why not the evil grandkids at gravesites holding their hands out in greed
Why do people like this don't feel as much hurt and suffering
Why does it seem my life is just a living offering?

i am not you

Stephanie Lynn Maxwell

I've come to find the final conclusion that I will never be
who you want me to be
That I will never do as you ask in the manner of which you asked it;
therefore, I will just not do it at all
I will never fulfill your dreams of a magnificent woman
unless, I'm compared to someone of lesser value
I will never stop crying because I will ever stop hurting
and maybe that's why the little girl in me will never grow up

Reaching

The Chart House

Brian Patrick

Plodding, trudging, slogging through the reeds
Praying for death, or at the very least – rescue
Sweat and muck mingle as one
Sliding down my face and pouring over my body

Why me? I have no repair
Looking behind; not a human in sight
The arrows fly by – whizzing in the dark
Into the mud I go – fearful

The light in the distance beckons
My limbs giving way to the weight
The rope catches my neck and tightens
Into the Chart House dragged to no avail

My captors start the endless mindless dance
I am at the beginning of my long goodbye
Dare I give them the dark secret they desire
Never, never …
… the blood trickles down my dirty neck.

The Poison

Brian Patrick

Insidious by its very nature
Yet soothing to those who indulge
It calls upon its broken cohort
Every two hours like a sentinel

It silently creeps along the mire
The Reaper within smiling and leering as he
Calls upon the Banshee McLemore
Searching for the wanton easy prey

Somehow the Poison drifts along the ebb
The shore becomes a winter haven
Solace among the rubble and waste
The storm as the background for living hell

The innocents have no fight with the
Pinprick that brings their body delight
Off into the realm of self edification
The gentle familiar warmth that overtakes

The warmth that turns into stark heat
Fluttering eyes look to the heavens
The beauty that is McLemore, lips waiting
Death in all its beauty awaits

To be stolen from the claws of McLemore
Cheated from the Reaper's blade
The spray that awakens the departed
Another snatched from the clutches of the Poison...
                                    ...has risen

The Damn Throb

Brian Patrick

My head pounds with each beat of my heart
The pounding grows with every second that passes
Seconds turn into eternities of distress
That distress grows into pain beyond endurance

The pounding continues to drain my spirit – hah
Pills and drink only mask what is happening in my head
Throbbing, throbbing, throbbing
My thoughts are turning inward – dastardly thoughts

The throbbing won't leave my head – it's ever-present
The darkness growing inside with every beat of my heart
Thoughts, gruesome thoughts, start to take form in the psyche
They churn and grow into such images of despair and worthlessness

A .38 feels so real, and yet so cold, in my trembling hand
Blue steel should do the job and consummate the end
Swift flight through the jaw into my throbbing head
No more throbbing or pain, nor thoughts of demons – just serenity

Commando blade might be nice – to the jugular the deed is done
The slow drip allows me to contemplate my demise
To see those things that drove me to this end
Slowly easing into nothingness might be the way to end the pain

Whatever chosen method of demise – this earthly life betrayed
Shall allow this body to die and decay over the timeless cosmos
To end this stay that has tormented my means throughout my time
I cling no more to thoughts unreachable and painful...
... only to fall into requiem

The Cassock

Brian Patrick

Tall, knowledgeable, caring, jovial and holy
Respected by many; exalted by others
His road – the road that should be taken
Irish of course, but not of the old sod

The unattainable, becomes at once, attainable
Your reckoning lightened by his words
The Black Robe is a tale to be told by all who believe
Believers they may be, but not for ease of living life

He, The Black Robe, beckons you to seek his countenance
Consolation is offered within the folds of his robes
You accept the gift without hesitation of belief
Your belief in the blood sacrifice of the unbelievable

The comfort of refuse offered by The Cassock
Truly blackens with the deceit of the unholy
All too friendly for men and boys
The betrayal all too familiar for me

The Captain's Harlot

Brian Patrick

The Captain, the Mother and a Familiar Face
Amble into the anteroom of my dwelling
It was announced that the Familiar Face
Was to spend her time with me

The Familiar Face, a frosted Jackie Kennedy
Complete with skirt, jacket and pill box crown
The Familiar Face, a nose too large
Breasts too large as well

Once alone, the Familiar Face draws two highballs
One for her, one for me
Confused, not yet in my teens, I drink
The taste, not appealing, yet encouraged to drink more

The Familiar Face removes her jacket
Revealing a silky, creamy sleeveless blouse
She voices that she is stiff from her flight
A very come hither voice entices me to massage her neck

The Familiar Face unbuttons her blouse
Brassiered bullet-like breasts appear
My boyhood grows hard with each passing second
Unzipped, she releases my boyhood from its cave

My head is spinning, throbbing like n'er before
The Familiar Face slowly unhooks
She takes my boyhood and caresses her breasts
Suddenly, her tongue embraces me as I spill over the range

Somewhere I suppose the Captain is beaming
Somewhere I suppose the Mother careening
Somewhere I suppose the Father is seething
Somewhere I suppose my future is bleeding

The Goo

Brian Patrick

Enveloped in the dark fog of goo
Surrounded by the dank starkness
To be home where it wallows
My being satiated with nothingness

Depth – reaching for the beckoning hand
My arms are stretched beyond their limit
Hands gripping for salvation
The salvation sinks below the hell frost

Silky smooth and rich with calling
The goo oozes everywhere
It calls for me to become enveloped
The light, the doorway just beyond

Redemption from the dark ooze
Something yearned for; yet still so far
Legs unable to propel
Forever stuck in the goo

The Edge
Brian Patrick

Standing on the precipice of my life
Waiting for the darkness to creep in
Looking at my starving body and wondering why
The images punctuate my failed existence

The world never wanted my being
It gave me nothing
A nothingness that craved heeling
My mind collapses on itself

How did I come to this precipice?
Why didn't the gathering herd receive me?
There can be no answer to my misery
The edge beckons me closer

As the images seep in and out
The abyss waits for my empty soul
The edge calls for me
The edge is no more – I have given in

The Captain's Kiss

Brian Patrick

The Captain floats in my world like a vulture
Someone given the charge of protection
A Captain in a realm of fledgling would-be's
The leader of men, only leads his own desires

The bus stop – all too familiar
Waiting, waiting and waiting
The Captain arrived making headway to me
Cringing to no avail, his tongue breaches me

Shuddering and recoiling into the shower I go
Desperately wanting to cleanse myself
No, this would never be
The shower – only a place for the Captain to lead

The shower that dreadful sinful place
The Captain, in all his glory, waits for the bearer to be
The game begins – pumping and pumping
Until the Captain's desirous fire is out

The Well

Brian Patrick

So isolated
My being feels like lead
Groping, groping
My fingers raw with ripped flesh

Rotting, putrid air
Breathing becomes a burden
Walls keep closing in
Dark, dank and musky

The dirty bastard
The cunning shit that he is
Exiled me to this earthly dungeon
My sentence to be drawn by death

The constant murky mess
Sludge that seeps into every pore
Without forethought or feeling
Life without touch; death

The Island

Brian Patrick

Interesting, that someone like me
Someone who grew large on the street
Would have their very own private island
An Island where one could go, but never live

The Island is far from beautiful
The flora fauna are deplete from color
The water colorless and hard to the touch
Sand invades - making all heavy

Visiting my island becomes too often
It pulls me – no beckons me like a lover
To extend my stay never to retreat
Never to return to the life I live

Once on, the chills and tremors grow
Dripping with sweat only to give in to torment
No sunshine, only the darkness and despair of the island
My island delivers desperate comfort

Never do I want to leave – only always
My island; only for me to wallow about
Forever trying to leave this paradise lost
Only to find my island visit lingers on

The Gift

Brian Patrick

A gift is given without expectation of return
A gift is wrapped in anticipation
A gift can be hidden in finery
A gift is accepted without question or hesitation

A gift may be breath into life
A gift is a feeling beyond mere words
A gift brings joy and solace
A gift allows total abandon

My gift is beyond all expectations
My gift is tall, blonde and exquisite
My gift is the greatest promise of life renewed
My gift is totally mine without reservation

Thankful for my gift of love
Thankful for my gift of life
Thankful for my gift of beauty
Thankful for my gift of forever

Song of the Streets

Jazz Organs
Grace Black

Sitting upon the rocks we slipped
    names to each other
    drugs to each other
    instinctual intent
I intentionally chose
    not to speak of summer
    not to speak of the injustice of that dead cat
    on Fischer Boulevard
not to speak of
    Neptune's blue concentrated
    archetypal madness
not to speak of
    jazz organs
    because we only ever spoke about
    jazz organs
not to speak of
    the galactic realization I received
    staring at the ladybug on my shoulder
    which flew to the sky
    which flew to the sun
not to speak of
    the unknown realms where
    I traveled to in my sleep
    surrounded by red dust
    or that I'd rather be in the land of disappearing lights
not to speak of
    the fact that
    there were two cigarettes left and I squished them both
    when I slid down the cliff and scraped my knee
not to speak of
    the uncomfortable countenances
    of the church moms
    when confronted with concepts of

a homosexual agenda
   not to speak of
        platonic solids or
        the flower, the fruit, and the seed
        of life
  O big brother, O almighty solar logos
        give me something else to talk about
        besides jazz organs
        jazz organs
        jazz organs

Under the Eye of the Karma Lords

Grace Black

Under the eye of the karma lords
I fell
I died alone
holding tightly
a black obsidian stone

They picked up their pens
to inscribe my name
in the great Book of Life
"She Shall Pass"
ink black as eternity

I am no more than nothingness
I am no less than all
I am no longer a form
I am the center of a sphere

I am no longer here

When I'm Fine

Grace Black

When I'm fine, boy I tell ya
life is so grand
how did I end up in such a great city
I smile and I step in puddles
I myself am a puddle
I want nothing, I have all
my walk is a jazz piece,
my step is a snare
my voice is a saxophone
I sing to the pigeons
my socks feel just right on my feet
out of the shadow of a building
I stepped into the sun
The Earth spirit loves me
even though I drive a car
even though I step on the grass
she loves me and I'm fine

Trust

Grace Black

I	trust
your	hips
they	move
so	swift
the	future
I	can't
be	sure
of	this
but	oh
your	hips
they	move
so	swift

Sand Man

Grace Black

Your sand paper hands
on the small of my back

sand me down,
change my shape

to fit your hands
to fit your wish

I'll mold back to myself
in time

I always do

Floating

Grace Black

I was born
I float
I will die
I float
but I was not born, I was here all along
floating, floating, floating
Seems like everyone's picking a fight,
well, I pick to float
Some people think that they're in control
they're just floating
We're all just floating
some of us don't know it yet
they'll learn
But me, I've been floating all along
floating all alone
floating, floating, gone

The Land of Disappearing Lights

Grace Black

The land of disappearing lights
Glimmers in the distance
So amorous
So brilliant
But just when you get
Oh so close
EVANESCE –
It's gone, it was never there
Life is strange that way

Supernova

Grace Black

I want to be disease
I want to have control
I want decay
I want trees to rot
To remind me time is lost
To remind me time is there
I want bricks
Blowing in the wind
Everyone's an asshole
Everyone deserves a brick to the head
Everyone deserves to die
I have a trombone
Filled with cow guts
Play me a song
Play me that song you sing
In your head
When the world is moving too fast
And you want to get off
I want chaos
I want destruction of memories
I want to feel nothing
I want to burn cigarette holes in
Dead leaves
I want to leave
I want this poem dead

Horatio

Grace Black

My mother told me not to go
But she's fooled me once before
I'll listen nevermore

You took me to your sanctuary
You let me see your naked chest
I let you see mine
My dear and I we intertwined

Then you took the noose from my neck
And tied me to the sink
And lit a match

Now I'll never love again
My Horatio, sweet as sugar
Gave me only cavities

Fifth Dimension

Grace Black

In the fifth dimension
There is no such thing as working hard
Your desires are instantly manifest
What a place I'd like to be -
I'm so god damn lonely
For I can't be lonely in the fifth dimension
Where everything is One
How can I be lonely
When I'm all there is?
I don't want this body anymore
I want to be a star
Free from duality
I want angels to know my name
I want to break the cycle
Of birth and rebirth
For this body is dust
And to dust it shall return

Hung on the Sky

Grace Black

Sir, you got a light?
It's cold as hell tonight

I'm lonely again
The stars are on my side
I see no end in sight
The sky is so damned bright

My shoes scrape the pavement
I'm so methodic
The rhythm calms my brain
The brain you made so neurotic

Is that my breath I see?
Or smoke
Or both

My toes are so numb
I'm too hung
On the sky
To go inside

Meet You There
Grace Black

Does unconsciousness in this world
mean consciousness in another?

If you're not here, where did you go?

I saw a man
asleep in his chair
with his mouth exposed
eyes half closed

Where did he go?
Will I ever know?
I'll meet you there! I said
and pulled the sheets to my chin

When I woke up
I remembered nothing
of where I had been

I guess one can't have it both ways
it's this reality or that one

Dreamless, we sleep
It all disappears
Until we return
Where we're
Bound by gravity
Bound by body
Bound

Toxic

Empty

Jacqueline Flores

There was this girl
who wanted to be a boy
she lied to the one person
whom she claim(ed)
she truly cared for
her words were like galaxies
and she spilled back velvet
poisoning my mind with black holes – when I would ask her about herself
her mind was empty
with no answers
like the unanswered questions
about the
universe

I need to let go
Jacqueline Flores

I will be on your doorstep
waiting for a door that
I know won't open in a matter
of seconds, even years
you did love me
sometimes you still do
like in songs that you say
remind you of me
in poems you write in your
faded journal with initials
at the end that I don't know of

Now you've hidden goodbyes
at the tip of my tongue
and have printed white ink
"move on move on move on"
on a paper I won't ever dare to pick up

Each time I try to get you closer to me
you push me just a centimeter away
but centimeters soon turn into miles
but even miles away you're
still holding on to me
hurting me
maybe hurting yourself
by stretching your arms so far
soon your arm will numb and
let go from my delicate palm
and when you do
maybe I will be able to finally
let
    go of you too

A poem he wrote for me

Jacqueline Flores

I dream of your
              hugs,
                    kisses,
and I'm loyal to you in dreams
I dream of your smile
       and again I begin to
                  fall for you
I also dream that you realize that
I want to be a part of your world
I live in my dreams
and I want to wake up
and give you my real love . . .
              I'm tired of imagining
I want to wake up
  to make it come true
I always dream of you
I have no other option
Only like this my heart lives;
I dream that by your side
I can believe again
that I won't lose
But I just can't wake up

I hate you X2

Jacqueline Flores

I really do hate
how I see you as this
perfect human being
with a perfect beautiful mind
and you really don't deserve that because you're the worst
you grew poisonous flowers in my rib cage; poisoned me with your mind
drowned me in a deep blue sea and
left me there when you were done

wrists (10w)

Jacqueline Flores

> My wrists are crying puddles
> maybe they miss you too

4/14/14

Jacqueline Flores

I don't know why I love u so much
you don't even show me
the love I need
the affection I would like
to have from you
I can't feel your touch
I can't feel anything
just the words you say and write
and your voice that, oh boy, that I love
so dearly which keeps me awake
through the cold lonely nights
the voice that I lose sleep to
and the words that I cry to
and it's not that I want to feel
a little weak from another
human being
I just cry
like my body is begging me to cry
like my eyes just turn teary and
water runs down my face
the way it runs down the windows that night I guess the rain
reminds me of you
and how you are sensitive like the water touching the windows so softly
making beautiful kinds of droplets
but, oh boy, all I ask is please don't
ever leave me and be by my side
come to me and
hold me like you did with her
stop filling my rib cage with
false butterflies

just love me like you loved her
and show me the love
you wish you showed her earlier
just please let me be her or
at least pretend so I can feel happy
because you're my happiness
and I know . . . oh I know that
that's the worst thing someone
can do to themselves

Leave me

Jacqueline Flores

If I don't make you laugh on your worse days if I'm not the one that you
go to when you don't want to speak to another human being
if I don't put a smile on your face
just by you listening to my voice
If I don't make your heart skip a beat
when I say I love you
leave me
If I'm not on your mind 24/7
maybe even less
(so it can be an exception)
and if my name is not on your school notebooks with hearts on it
(maybe my name in a light grey)
leave me
run away from me
far, far away
if the thought of you not wanting to speak to me again crosses your path
on days you hate me
leave me
if I don't make you squirm in happiness
even if it's just by the simple word
of hello
and make you the saddest when I say
the simple words of just good bye
leave me
just please leave me
just please do so
because you deserve better and
there is someone out there
who will make you feel
the way I wish I could
so leave me

Don't date a poet

Jacqueline Flores

Don't ever fall in love with a poet
They will indeed watch your every move and admire
they will write about how the pen marks on your finger when you write
don't ever because they will trace
every single freckle you have on
your face and write about the color of each and every one of them and
describe how they smile so brightly
under the sunlight they will want you
to want to know every little thing about them even if it's just what hand
they write with and want you
to be wondering why they write with that specific hand when in
reality it doesn't even matter
the poet will watch the way you dig
your eyes onto that book and your small quick remarks onto the 26 letters
all crumpled together and will know that every day at 5:28 you smile
they will look deeply into your eyes
to see if they can at least take a little
peek of your soul and they will write
about you like if you were the only
thing they see good in this world
they will want to know what you think
about when you look at them and
see if you also count each and
every freckle and hope and write
that you do but they will
love you endlessly and they will
show you they love you and only you but don't date a poet if you aren't
capable to watch them and
admire their imperfections
when they sleep at night
beside you

Want
Jacqueline Flores

I just want somebody who wants
to taste my mind at 3 am
who doesn't get annoyed by my jealousy and by me texting them
in all caps when I'm happy and
texting them 6 times in a row
someone I can walk with at the park
and stay 5 hours on the swings
just laughing and talking about anything that pops up onto our minds
somebody who isn't afraid to catch me when I fall for them
I want someone who
kisses my forehead
holds my hands and
never wants to let go
I want someone who knows me
inside and out and
knows what I'm thinking just
by glancing at me
someone I can sing along
to the radio with
someone who chooses me over anyone else
and doesn't think twice about it

I just really want that to be you

don't/do come back

Jacqueline Flores

I wish you would lie to me
once more
and say I love you
(**please**) do as I say and lie to me
I know you can read this
and when you do
(if you ever do)
this is your sign of please don't (**come**) back
don't put me under your skin again
don't put me in the (**back**) of your thoughts again
don't hurt me

(**to**) infuse poison into my veins was one thing
but to let (**me**) die for you instead of falling
knowing we weren't for one another was another thing

left

Jacqueline Flores

I love you so much

so I gave up on you
stopped talking to you
and watched you love somebody else

and even though I know I am miserable and so sad not speaking to you

I know I am so much better off
without you

i hate you

Jacqueline Flores

I ripped these poems out just as roughly
as you ripped me from your heart
I hate how
you're the blood to my veins
the good to my bye and
I really hate how you grew poisonous flowers in my rib cage
how you entered me like nicotine and
how my lungs are now filled with a grey dark cloud

don't you ever dare say that you never felt anything and
that I once wasn't the light of your life and
that I didn't know anything about you
because we were strangers who
knew each other very well

I loved you more than the sea loves the shore
and you drowned me in a beautiful deep blue sea

Replace

Jacqueline Flores

I should have known that
when you said I was the moon and
you were the stars

that the moon is soon replaced by the sun

finally
Jacqueline Flores

I feel like this is coming to an end
I can see the curtains closing into darkness
and I don't know why I haven't cried
like I would have a few weeks ago

I know we did love with full aching hearts and
I know it hurts to say goodbye
but I'm still asking myself
why haven't I come crawling back to you yet?

Maybe I am finally learning
not to love you and
Maybe I am finally falling out of love
just like you did

i need to stop wondering

Jacqueline Flores

I'm really anxious to scribble about you because
it makes me feel everything that you make me feel
and everything feels so much more honest and sincere
when my words smudge up against
the side of my palm and dye it blue
as my pen dashes to keep up with my heart and tears

but don't want it to be honest and sincere
or feel that way anymore
because I thought I was moving on
moving on from ache
that I wish I didn't crave
I thought I knew all of this was
unwise and non-realistic

but maybe I need to stop thinking
and just let myself feel;
feel the goose bumps you give me,
feel the pain you give to my wrists,
feel the blood you infuse into my veins and
all the blood I let out of my veins because of you

but maybe I don't need to know everything,
like exactly what you're thinking
or exactly how I feel
maybe even exactly how you feel
or how all of this is going to turn out -
I already have an idea of how it will turn out to be;
I don't even need to have an idea
I just need to let it be and
whatever happens, happens

Everything isn't always going to be clear,
and not everything is going to be given to you by hand
and you'll always have to work for what you want
and let go of everything that makes you anxious;
you know that at the end you will be pleased with just
loving yourself
not just by loving you, who doesn't love me

I'd like to be able to leaf through the trees and smile
even if you are not there, wandering beside me

i want

Jacqueline Flores

(**I**) think my biggest fault was
wanting to know everything
that was yet to cross my mind
I want to know everything you feel
at any given moment
what you (**wish**) for when the clock hits 11:11
(**I**) want you to want me to know why
you painted your bedroom walls dark blue
(**was**) it that the day you picked the bucket of paint
you saw the sea really dark and you wanted to feel free and wild?
(**on**) the day of your birthday do you feel older?
I want to know (**your**) fears and
which day of the week you feel happiest on
and what's on your (**mind**)
before you close your eyes into darkness
But most of all
I want to know everything you feel
even just by me glancing at you

idk

Jacqueline Flores

The way cold water hisses when it starts to boil
the same way butterflies start to build up
just by your eyes simply passing right through me

I just wish I wasn't a tree
when a hurricane passes by

robber

Jacqueline Flores

you broke into my home
searching for anything that can be
easily grabbed
you got a hold of my heart
stole it and just as easy as it was to get
was how easy you ran away with it
I never got a hold of your precious face
you just kept on running -
you kept that mask on

even when I got a hold of your heart as well

Him

Jacqueline Flores

No matter who you are, just know that I'll always love you
   and you'll always be in my heart.
I'll always consider you the first person I've ever caught true feelings for,
   never will I know
the answers to the many questions about you
   but I hope someone walks into your life and
takes your breath away the way I couldn't. I'll forever love you
   no one can ever love you
the way I can, but I hope that one person that can, comes along
soon
   I do believe you
deserve love in your life not the love you made me give you.
   I'll always want you more than
you'll ever want me and that's okay because love doesn't exist
   only one can love on and the
one they love will always love someone else much more
   and you love someone else much
more than you'll ever love me. I hope you do one day fall in love
   if you haven't already. I hope
she touches you much more than just your body. You've hurt me so much
   but I love you so
much that no matter how deeply you cut my skin
I still want the best for you. You always say
that "God puts people in your life for a reason and they leave for a reason."
   but you'll never
know the reason as to why I got into your life and that is what happens
   when in reality we
aren't meant for one another

you're my drug

Jacqueline Flores

when i was just a child and didn't know any better
i would speak to strangers and let them
whisper into my ear little secrets about you

they told me the good things and not the bad
things i had to figure out on my own
that eventually you can be as addictive

as the baggies that you gave me in the
corner of the street

Eyes in the Aspens

Dead Inside
Daniel Smith

Wake up screamin' in the middle of the night
I taste the bile that's starting to rise
And know that I'm in hell again
'Cause the zombie mother fuckers are screamin' outside
More real than the demons in my own mind
And maybe I should let them in
'Cause the world's already been eatin' at my brain
And everything I've done has been in vain
So dead inside is all I am
With all the human monsters drainin' me
Feedin' on my pain and misery
I'm already feedin' the damned

Tonight I'll die without you
You can't control my demise
I'll suffer well without you
I'm already dead inside

I open up the door and walk to the end
Of the drive and my life, where my new friends
Are just like me, so dead inside
I welcome them and their cold embrace
And smile as the blood pours down my face
Their teeth the last thing through my mind
I wake with a hunger like never before
And find I have never wanted anything more
Than feeding on the living brain
My asshole neighbor's still asleep in his bed
He wakes up screaming as I empty his head
That bastard died in horrible pain

Tonight I live without you
I can't control my appetite
I'll feed my pain without you
I am dead inside

It seems each victim wears your face
And now a thought I can't erase
I'm wasting this gift I've been given
I leave a bloody trail right to your door
And find you huddled up on the floor
Regrettin' the life you're barely livin'
You see it's me and start to scream
As a feeling so much better than any dream
Comes as I taste the waste inside your head
I smile as the life inside you fades
And the pain you've been feeding on starts to invade
Just like me, you are the living dead!

Tonight, I have devoured you
I've become your demise
I have finally shown you
What it's like to be dead inside

Your misery becomes you
So lost and empty inside
I've given what I owe you
Just like me, you're dead inside

Slumber

Daniel Smith

The only thing that changes
Is that nothing stays the same
There's always some new way
We find we're buried in the pain
Someday, we will find
The happiness that we desire
But now, we suffer sweetly
As we stumble through the fire
We choke on smoke of memories
And battles we have lost
Even when we win
We find that losing is the cost
Choking on the hopes
That keep us holding out for more
Wanting something, anything
To numb us to the core
When will we find everything
That we've been looking for?
Nothing left but nothing
I can't take this anymore
Rip this broken heart out
Of the darkness in my chest
And give me just one moment
For my weary soul to rest
I know the day will come
When everything will be all right
If I can only make it through
This one dark, hellish night

But even sleep won't make it so
To unconsciousness I go
To the land of pleasant nightmares
Where the winds of change still blow

May my slumber bring the end
To living hell, where I'm condemned
Where no amount of dreams
Can make this waking nightmare end

So wide awake
In this land of disenchantment
This disease
Slowly poisoning my heart
I can't fake this anymore
This pain that I've commanded
Everything I've never done
All the things that I've done wrong
I've tried so hard
To be the man I long to be
Watching every selfless action
Fashioned into my demise
I can't take this anymore
My every waking moment
Now consuming every reason
I have left for holding on
I want to end this pain
But I don't want to leave this world
With so many battles raging
Just to save my weary smile
I won't take this anymore
My life I'm not forsaking
I just want to rest my heart for a while

But even sleep won't make it so
To unconsciousness I go
To the land of pleasant nightmares
Where the winds of change still blow
May my slumber bring the end
To living hell where I'm condemned

Where no amount of dreams
Can make this waking nightmare end

Everything that's come before
Has taught me that persistence
Is the key, and holding on
Sometimes means letting go
Everything that's now in store
Is silently insisting
That I give myself over
To the pain that lives inside
I won't break like times before
Your words won't devastate me
'Cause your life is not in order
How the hell can you live mine
You can't see what's on the inside
'Cause you can't see past that shell
You only hate me
'Cause you hate who you've become
You've fooled yourself, you know
Your lies now have control
You're the only one believing
Just how all of this will go

I won't take this anymore
I won't do this anymore
I won't let you break my heart

So you can soothe your empty soul
I'm tired of your lies
You still can't hear my cries
You can't even see what's coming
By my sweetly twisted smile
You've fastened your own cell
This is over; this is hell

Your black and bleeding heart
Will surely stay with me a while

My hate will make it so
To your level I now go
I can be your living nightmare
Since your heart has turned to stone
May my words now bring an end
To living hell, where you pretend
That every lie you've spoken
Makes you happy in the end
Even sleep won't rest your soul
For unconsciousness, I know
Can twist your waking nightmares
'Til they spin out of control
I hope the truth will bring an end
To every lie that you pretend
And bring redemption to your hollow heart
So you can love again

When Angels of Darkness and Light Fall
Daniel Smith and Collaborator

Light...

Walking blindly through the dark, hearing no sound. I reach out for you, grasping for your warmth. You're nowhere to be found. I'm blind and I'm lost. Lost within the dark woods of your soul. I want your warmth; the touch of your hands. The feel of your lips against mine. Yet, I feel nothing. Nothing but the coldness of where you used to be. The coldness of alone. Alone and shivering with the anticipation of finding you once more. But, for now I wander through these woods, fighting the darkness and whatever may lurk within. I will find you, search and fight until my heart beats no more. I sit thinking of you, thinking of the morbid array of thoughts that swim through that beautifully twisted mind of yours. You appeal to me. The darkness of your soul delights me. I love the anticipation of the next sick and twisted thing that will slip through those beautiful lips of yours. The attraction to you consumes my every being. Consumes me for everything I ever have or ever will be.

Darkness . . .

I savor the flavor of a thousand delights found in one single moment when your twisted smile lights the shadow of time to the core of emotion, leaving me more complete with every instance, and a little less myself each time we part, anticipating every next moment together in madness, lunacy, and contentment.

Light . . .

I bask in the ambiance of your soul. I bathe in the light of your eyes. I devour each word that falls from your lips. Every moment spent together I die some inside knowing that you'll never be mine. I'll never be the one to feel the warmth of your lips, the tenderness in your kisses. Never feel the ecstasy in which I so desire. You shall never be mine, yet the torment of being around you draws me in ever so much more. I may never have you to call my own, so I will satisfy my own needs by looking into your eyes, by hopelessly clinging to every word. Loving someone who never will be mine will be my death. A death I so willingly accept.

Darkness . . .

So we collide and coincide on opposite plateaus of the same parallel, a product of storms never raged, battles never won, and pleasures never quenched, holding moments passed in equal satisfaction as those that may have been, as the imploding loss of unknowing melds the two into one final entity, more powerful than the feeling of gratitude for all of the powers that be for giving us the one thing no one could ever replace . . . the penetrating ecstasy orbiting about this world of our own creation, to revel in every moment together, and suffer every second torn apart, in time, and in mind.

Light . . .

We wander through the dark, hand in hand. I feel your supple lips brush my cheek. I turn to look into your eyes once more when I realize you have changed. Your soul has become dark. Your eyes have become cold. I'm afraid of you now. Afraid of your touch, of your love. I try to turn from you, to get away, but you hold on tight. Your grasp on my hand sends shivers up my spine. I need to be free of you, to get away from you to save my own soul from being lost into the new darkness which has become you.

Darkness . . .

I'm lost within the shadows cast by every inner demon, unraveling their chaotic waltz to the symphony of my pain. I turn to whisper my deepest secret, my lips trailing the ghosts of my heart's desire upon your cheek, and realize it can never come to pass, turning before the very words can die upon breath now sustaining me in suffocation. I grasp your hand more tightly, magnifying the tremors in my own, as the fear of losing myself without you intensifies. I need to be free of you, if only to save you from the darkness now contaminating the waters of my soul, for how can you be my heart's salvation if it means the damnation of your own soul as you descend with me into oblivion? How can I whisper when shouts of madness waver upon my tongue? How can I speak my heart and my fear when such a morbid chorus drowns out my sanest of thought, turning my emotions into a chaotic lesson in confusion and eminent danger? I see my future, far more clearly than my past, for every memory made without you is one I would give my soul to forget, knowing I would die in vain, for the memories we favor the least haunt us more vividly than the happiest of moments could ever dare imagine. The choice between fading alone in unending torment and dying with you by my side, suffering in silence as I scream absurdities upon the dying wind is simple. Living without you is my eternal hell. So easy to fall in love. So hard to stand alone.

Light . . .
Only always is what you told me. Only always will you be there. Only always will you care. Only always will you only have eyes for me. Only always do you lie. Only always do you cause me pain. Only always do you inflict such dire emotions in me that I can no longer bare. Only always will I die by your touch. Only always, my love.

Darkness . . .
Only always will I be so calm in my insanity. Only you will always be the one to draw the best from me. Only always will I dare to drown in nothingness compared to every thought you only always bring to mind, each time I stare into the void that lies between what's real and only memory of things that only always never come to pass between the glass refraction, only always cutting swiftly to the bone, condemning me to hold on to words that only always go unspoken. Only always will I be broken, bleeding upon the foundations of souls forever seeking completion, only always incomplete. Only always alone. Everything I've tried to find inside a dark and weary world, I find in your eyes, within your words, within your soul. The interwoven feelings of contentment and deprivation cradle me in confliction as I hold opposing worlds within my grasp, watching as they collide in euphoric tragedy, spawning chaos amidst a field of hauntingly menacing desires, blooming like undead roses from the devastation that my life once was, empowering loss with hope and regret, and the knowledge that, even though never to be mine own, such a thing, such a feeling, does, indeed, exist within a world so heartless and corrupt. Mine to behold, but never mine to hold for more than just a picture of what life can be . . . perfectly imperfect, and still possible for me.

Light . . .
You slowly caress my soul with the diseases on your tongue. How can one
fornicate such passion within the heart of a beast like me?

Darkness . . .
You stir within me the echo of desire, reverberating ironically throughout
my every thought, as the deepest part of me quivers with satisfaction.

Light . . .
A satisfaction I so desperately yearn for. The very essence of you makes
me quiver in this ironic state of bliss. Your body has become a metaphor
of emphasis for me.

Darkness . . .
I remain intoxicated, imbibing wine flowing from the beauty of your soul,
captivated by the fire tearing through my veins like molten glass with
every beat of my tormented heart, counting every second spent dreaming
in vain into its unrightful place upon the skin of eternity.

Light . . .
With nowhere to go, nowhere to hide, your words haunt my soul; haunt
every fiber of my being. Drown me in a flood of emotion that I cannot
seem to waiver. Your words flow through my body as the disease which is
you spreads to my core.

Darkness . . .
The very thought of the object of my idolatry imprisons me in thin air,
levitating over balance and corruption, wrestling two demons at once; that
which damns me with morality, and that which delivers me with the
anticipation of every mistake, crying to be born, to thrive, to be obeyed.
Take my hand. Set my heart free. Burn with me in depthless passion, void
of conscience, bursting at the seams with long suffered lust come to
fruition, calming every shrieking moan of absolution, losing our souls as
we have lost our minds, with violent denial, giving way to complete and
total gratification of knowing that although we suffer so well amidst all

that drags us further into hell fire, we suffer willingly in the greedy embrace of mutual condemnation.

Light . . .

The words that flow from your fingertips flow through me and reverberate through my mind into my soul. My soul which you are such a dire part. You who lifts me up when I am within inches of knocking upon Hell's hollow doors. You are the one who comforts me when I am mere inches away from taking my last breath. I will love you until the end of time. As you contemplate if I truly care, now that my heart pulsates on this flaccid plane of existence, and that you will always be one of the many reasons my heart will continue to thump its many beats. I reach for you, finding nothing but the coldness of where you were. This atrocity of life haunts me, ridiculing me for ever having loved you. The beast within me screams your name to no avail. I'm lost and alone without you near. Time has lost its meaning. I'm trapped in a void of nothingness. Wondering ever so much when you are going to set me free. Why won't you set me free? Crying amongst the pain you cannot feel. Tears disintegrate into the harshness of the rain. The validity of your words go once more unspoken. Hence once again the darkness has become the only reality in which I thrive. I mustn't relive the days amongst your lies. The lies you have spit at me with such callousness. The unspoken realm of my reality has become so clear, so vivid. I must be rid of you. Must free my soul from the snare you've captured me within. Yet the fire within your eyes has compelled me once more. For why must I fall into the depths of you?

Darkness . . .

Yet pain I do feel, for every time that I draw close, you drift further away even as your heart reaches for me. It is the rain itself that disintegrates into the harshness of the tears I shed in longing for the day when you understand that my words are pure and not some greedy guise, for the darkness wherein you dwell is but the shadow that your doubt casts upon your weary heart? If it had all been a lie, then why do the memories that so torment you ring so true, more savagely with every second that passes in which we are not drowning in each other's arms? It be not untruth, but frustration that empowers my words, for the very thought of life without you is only the precursor to my living hell. The reality of all is that you are my life and you are my death, sustaining me and suffocating in equal measure, imbibing my heart with your very essence, and rending it asunder with every tear you shed in unbelief. If you must be rid of me, then do so quickly, and have pity upon my tormented soul, for I wish not for you to fall into the depths of my sorrow, but to fall with me as I fall into the undying beauty that is you.

The Door That Is Not A Door
Daniel Smith

A window that is no window at all
Shows a vague view of my soul.
Coated with grime of misfortune and time,
It does not dilute what is shown.
Such evils I've done, and deeds I recall
All take a murderous toll.
The after effects of my ways and my crimes
Leave alien landscapes, unknown.
There is a door that is not a door
Which opens on nothing and everything.
There is a key that is not a key
That unlocks, but never obeys.
Oh, such a chore to tread the dirt floor,
And not disturb dust of remembering
The days we were free, now imprisoned, you see,
In a cell of our ignorant ways.
There is a mind long hidden behind
This door that is not a door.
A whisper in time, and shadow of doubt
Locked away in a trunk of denial.
But there, in a mirror of cobwebs, we find
Like always and never before,
That life limps along, and Death gives a shout,
As all of our thoughts go on trial.
In fist is this key, which is not a key,
Screaming to ruin my life.
To go forth and unlock all things now confined
And drown me in things that once were.
I now see that freedom does not make you free
When yourself you imprison in strife.
The voices are never far gone from my mind,
As tragedy begs to occur.

I fear to discard this key not a key,
For it may find another's hand
Whose curiosities for morbid restraint
May exceed those of my will to change.
The door not a door will be opened in me,
The trunk split apart on command.
Regardless of effort, and numb to complaint,
A return to the prisoner, deranged.
So madness, you see, resides within me
Behind the door not a door.
Madness remains beyond cold shell, as well,
Forced by the key not a key.
Forged to be keeper of insanity
By my hand and others before,
By my hand or another, I walk through this hell.
One price or another, I'll never be free.

Ruination
Daniel Smith

Spasmodically chaotic
Flies the embryonic tonic
Through the veins and to the brain
Heart and soul are now defiled
Complicating, hating
Imitating, devastating
Dying stars so full of scars
Schizophrenia's inner child

Ash to ash and dust to dust
Sanity begins to rust
Bleeding laughter
From beneath the mourner's veil
Carried on into the dawn
Imprinted on the demon spawn
Unresting and ingesting
The dismembered and impaled

The bones of the alone
Rattle on in monotone
Resurrecting and collecting
Tortured ghosts of minds depraved
Humanity receding
Feeding on the need for bleeding
Leaving mental catacombs
Eternally engraved

Neverafter

Daniel Smith

Here in the Neverafter
I have seen the things you won't show
It's such a sweet disaster
Just how much our love could have grown
But I can taste the emptiness
That lies behind each smile you fake
And I can feel your hate infest
Watching every move you won't make
And it's not that I don't love you
It's not that I don't care
It's just that I have seen your every microscopic layer
Despite what you may think, I'm not afraid of being alone
But I am afraid that you'll suffocate my soul
Because I've already died a thousand times
With every time you never said "I love you" first
And I've bled a million tears
With every day that you've been so far from my side
I'm haunted by the memories of who you used to be
Before your lies became perverse
And I'm chocking on the ashes
Of the love you threw away
Before I left you so far behind
And the stories of the person
That you never used to be
Like an echo in a graveyard
Of a love that could not be
And the mourning of the people
We never could have been
There's a story never told here
It's the one of you with me

Silence Speaks

Daniel Smith

Silence is a hard thing to understand. It has a wide vocabulary, and sometimes rings out so loudly, as if a choir of confusion, that it is nearly impossible to translate. Sometimes it is so void of life that one cannot even hear one's own heart beating. Silence is never the same twice, for it comes with different emotions and circumstances each time, even if seemingly the same, and it always has something new to unravel, whether it is what we need to hear, what we refuse to hear, or what we've been waiting to show, or trying not to show, ourselves or another, all along. Silence can be an ever changing friend, or an unrelenting enemy. No matter the form or fashion, silence is, and will forever remain, the most welcome and unwanted part of our lives.

It is an often overlooked truth that silence can be anything but. The voices echoing within the vastness between one ear and the next are still far more audible than anything exhaled amidst a mixture of lips, teeth, and tongue, so that even when we are not speaking our mind, the mind is speaking, even if only to the soul attached to it, speaking volumes silently as they translate into emotion and action, or the lack thereof, creating a vocabulary of gesture and expression, but also of stillness and blankness, woven together in both intricacy and complication, losing nothing in translation of language, but sometimes losing much in the heart's translation of emotion to and from a soul other than its own.

Emotions are each a different language in themselves, for each has their own gestures, expressions, and blank stillness. The mind learns new languages by hearing and reading and teaches the mouth and fingers to translate from thought to spoken or written word, and it depends upon the exposure and the depth of study and experience in any given language as to which we become more or less fluent in, both in speaking and in understanding. It is much the same with the heart. It learns each new language of emotion by the experience of feeling, and depending on the depth and experience with each, the heart becomes more fluent in some over others, and sometimes one over any other. It is the relationship between the mind and the heart that truly allows us to understand these feelings, in others as well as in ourselves.

We say that it is the heart that guides us. We say to follow our hearts. We say that our heart has been broken, or that it has been made whole. We say that our heart hurts, our heart leaps, skips a beat, races, that it swells and that it grows cold, or one of any other descriptive analogies. It is often what we feel inside our chest that dictates what we decide upon in our minds in any given thing of emotional importance. Poetry, literature, art, everyday speak, and even actions and expressions project and profess what it is that we feel in our hearts at any given instance or in any given circumstance. This is merely the hearts reaction to what our minds perceive in any given emotion of circumstance.

It is the depth of the understanding of any given thought or idea, fact or fiction, that ties into the emotional in any way or on any level for each of us. Depending upon what we think and believe about any given thing, it will have a different reaction in each of us depending on how important or unimportant it may be to each of us based on our individual way of thinking. The differences between what each of us considers important or unimportant has an influence on how each of us feels about any given thing or circumstance. It is our feelings about what and how we think and what we understand (or sometime believe what we understand) that are the basis, the origins, the essence of or emotions.

The mind could not function if not for the heart performing its own function. In turn, the heart could not function if not for the mind. They are dependent upon one another. They are slave to one another. As long as the two continue to function together in any conscious state of awareness (or in some unconscious states), the mind literally controls heart and the heart literally sustains and obeys the mind. The mind may decipher and understand what the heart feels in reaction to its thoughts, but it is the heart that feels it. This is why we speak of the heart and not the mind in almost every instance of emotion. This however, does not mean that everyone's mind understands the heart's obedience to the emotions created by the thoughts it produces, just as most do not realize it is the heart's physical reaction in emotion that the mind relates its thoughts and feelings knowingly and descriptively. This lack of understanding applies more to emotions emanating from others, be they audible or silent, than they do to the emotions we feel ourselves the greater percentage of time.

How can this be so? How is it that the majority of the time, we misread, ignore, or completely overlook the emotions emanating from others when we feel those same emotions ourselves, and often express them in the same ways, whether more or less often, and whether we show our emotions deliberately, or they show despite our failed attempts at masking or hiding them? How is it that we fail to understand, or understand more fully, the torment or elation anyone other than ourselves can be going through at any given moment when we, ourselves, have been through the same or similar circumstances? Even when we have not been through the same circumstances bringing about such emotions in others, how is it that we have such a hard time understanding that the same emotions we experience can be brought about in others by completely different circumstances?

Maybe it is the amount of people who fake emotions to gain for themselves something from another in ill begotten ways so often that it becomes hard to believe what so many try to show or hide from us emotionally. Maybe it is that we are so often trying to understand those things in and for ourselves that we fail to see how those emotions affect others in their interactions with us and in their own lives. Maybe it is where some of the circumstances that bring about the same emotions for others are not quite the same circumstances that bring them about for us at times. Maybe it is where we are in a different state of emotion at times than the person or people we are interacting with, and our absorption in our own emotions takes our sight and understanding away from theirs at any given moment. It could be any one or more of these reasons, or even that we have had our own emotions misread and disregarded so many times that our own emotions have become so deep and ominous at times, that we cannot see through the shadows that surround us or the elation we feel for ourselves in those moments. There are so many reasons that could be factors.

Even if we don't feel the same emotions at the same exact time as someone else, or for the same exact reasons, we still feel the same emotions as everyone else, for despite each emotion being a different language, what we feel is universal. Despite the false witnesses of emotion who seek to deceive for whatever gain or manipulation they so choose, there are still so many good people trying to understand themselves, as well as others. In emotion, regardless of race or nationality or origin, we all speak the same emotional languages, even if some of us are more fluent in some emotions over others due to our personal experiences. If more of us would try, and some of us would try harder, to understand the emotions of others, not only from the circumstances bringing them to life, but in the effect each emotion has on each person in their moments of emotion, just as we so try to understand our own, then maybe, just maybe, there would not be so much confusion, misunderstanding, and in some cases, judgment, at the differences in what others feel and experience in any moment, whether similar or the same to our own, and hearts would heal more so than being broken, and we would see similarities over differences.

Despite how we live, where we come from, and who each of us are personally, we are all the same in what we feel in our hearts and through our minds, and in our differences, we are still one in the same. Our minds control our hearts, and our hearts control our minds. We all feel, and we all feel the same, even if at different times than one another. Even when there are no words to say, and even when our words won't bleed upon page or screen, or our emotions will not translate to whatever medium of expression we choose, our silence still speaks just as loudly as our words, for our every thought and action is based upon the language of emotion, and in that, we all speak the same language, even in silence.

Where it is so often that silence from another, or reflected upon another, determines our own understanding and emotion in interaction with the emotions of others, we should listen and try to understand more than just cursory what those silences reflect emotionally. Sometimes, our silences speak just as much, if not more, than words or other mediums can allow, if we would but listen as closely in others as we do in ourselves in the languages of emotion, with our hearts and minds in equal measure, instead of letting our own emotions in our own circumstances at any given time impede or disrupt how we see or hear these emotions effecting others in their own circumstances, similar or differing, for they are something we should try to relate to, not self-sidedly compare to our own in trying to self-deceptively prove that no one understands how we feel.

Beautiful Tragedy

Daniel Smith

Beautiful tragedy, you suffer sublime
As you fall from the twenty-fifth floor
Feelings of agony and wasted regret
Will soon be a burden no more
Tears that you shed in this ungrateful life
Will never discredit your face
Hatred will never be able to touch you
Nor will I, once you're gone from this place
Yet I suffer in silence as you fall away
Drawing closer to ending your pain
And I wonder if I could have loved you more deeply
If we were not going insane
But seconds stretch out to an endless abyss
As the love we have shared fills my mind
And I know that I lost you before you were lost
Because of what was left behind
Did I reach out to stop you as you stood there dying,
Or did I push you to the end?
Did I calm all your fears or instill fear inside?
Was I enemy or was I friend?
Did I show you the beauty that lies within nothing,
Or the ugliness in all you saw?
Could I have done more to bring joy to the madness,
Or joined you as you took the fall?
Why do I stand here and watch you fade out
When we could descend side by side,
And let the whole world pass us by just like always?
Together, to live and to die
But as seconds reclaim the time they're allotted
And choices begin to take toll
I watch in great wonder, forgetting my woes
As beautiful black wings unfold

Beautiful tragedy beginning to rise
Above a cruel world so cold
Overcoming her pain and erasing the stains
This cruel world did inflict on her soul
Turning to me as she rises above
She reaches out her scarred hands
I long to embrace her, my beautiful tragedy
Together, forgiven or damned
I step to the edge of the beckoning void
As I take my last breath in this hell
My eyes upon her as the world falls away
And the bars fall away from my cell
Seconds once again stretch out unending
As worlds collide in my mind
Memories fill me, for better or worse
I know that the worst is behind
I feel the release of a thousand mistakes
Taking flight as I now start to rise
I now hold the hands of my beautiful tragedy
As we break free of our broken lives
We chance to look down on a crowd gathered round
A pair of unfortunate souls
Twisted and broken, somehow hand in hand
As they met on the pavement below
An end to the pain brought on by a world
That somehow refused to care
Such wasted lives . . . a beautiful tragedy
So lost in love and despair

Thiever of Souls
Daniel Smith

Slow creeping castles in mind intertwine
With memories bled deeply with pain
Chaotic structures, foundations of fear
And lives of a dark crimson stain
Slivered intentions thrust deeply within
Black fingers which clutch death like gold
Breeding disfigured delusions of life
In a worm-ridden heart love can't hold
Distorted figures of flesh and of shadow
Vehemently spawning delusion
Embedded far within failure-worn skin
With morbid intent the intrusion
Tragedies breeding disease and a hunger
Consuming a weak self-control
Raging insanity, loss of humanity
Ravenous Thiever of Souls

**

Dust of a shadowed and well hidden ignorance
Envelopes discarded hope
Enhancing the feelings of failure and worthlessness
Of the lost soul who can't cope
More of the lessoning of love for life
Less of a reason for living
Imprisoned inside a one-sided world
Oppressor of self, unforgiving
So few the caring, supporting, and loving
Too many workers of pain
Within his mind, now void of forgiveness
Only one option remains
So few would mourn, so many rejoice

One bullet could cure this disease
Misguided hand holding cold false deliverance
Moves toward disaster with ease

Trembling fingers now pushing destruction
Begin to draw false freedom nigh
Conscience is screaming, imprisoned by hopelessness
Drowned out by suicide's lie
The kiss of cold steel, and death gives a whisper
As barrel is pressed against skin
The moment forgotten as soul-piercing words
Explode far more near than within
"Such a loss you endure. Such sorrow and pain.
Such a fool to think death sets you free."
Now a figure before, a shadow with substance
Dark whisper upon bended knee
Somewhat from fear, somewhat from awe,
Somewhat from thought hypnotized
The gun falls away, along with intentions
In company of undead eyes

Darkness leans closer, distorting a smile
Veiling intent with concern
Stretching its hand toward the vacant young man
Saying, "Come. There are things you should learn."
Contact is made, and light is betrayed,
As both fall down into the gloom
The young man awakens to heartless abandon
To learn of revenge in his tomb
"Your pain can end by ending the source,
And multiple sources there are.
Each individual judging your life
Leaves on your soul a new scar.
Erase every scar, and restore who you are
By sending their souls here to me.

Ask not what I do, and my promise to you
Is revenge will soon set you free."

Of all of the thoughts now inside his head
The victor is "ending the pain"
Tired of being the subject of scorn
Tired of going insane
"Kill them all. Yes. And, why not?" he concludes
"They've been killing me for years.
An end to the torment, an end to the pain,
An end to all of the tears."
Gaze fixed on eyes alive with death
Eager for cold recompense
The young man sells his soul with, "I will."
Darkness smiles. "Let us commence."
A savage young man, now barely a man
Arises to set himself free.
Not knowing he's fashioning his personal cell
With Darkness now holding the key

Cover of night and a murderous silence
Welcome the newborn disease
Un-natural sight on this victory night
Grants the new killer great ease
Now there is flight, cut loose from earth's ties
To soar into vengeance untold
And a hunger for more than was bargained for
As morbid desires unfold
All taken in with more pleasure than fear
More weapons with which to wage war
First there was only the goal to take life
Now there is drunkenly more
"They will endure much more physical pain
Than that which they carved on my soul."
And madness begins as delusion abounds

In the Slave to the Thiever of Souls

To the first window, the first scar of pain
Laid out on a bed of fine white
The falsified whore, who pretends to adore him
While taking new lovers each night
A trick of the fist, and a flick of the wrist
And teeth burrow into the flow
The life that once thrived on the tainting of lives
Now lost in irony's throw
As the well runneth dry, the Slave gives a cry
As the torture intended is lost
Yet the hunger now maddeningly cries from inside
To be silenced whatever the cost
Turning away as emptiness grows
More wicked than torture's regret
Vowing the next will experience pain
Before their life's blood has been let

The next pair of scars, so distinct under stars
Together, as in his despair
The father and mother of what he once was
For him they had never been there
"Break them apart in each other's view,
Then hang them with their own entrails."
But ravenous hunger devours the thought
As self-treachery is unveiled
Before realizations of torture now lost
Has time to fully set in
The two have been drained, their life now contained
In the ravenous nothing within
The Slave is consumed by rage beyond end
As the hunger continues to grow
Revenge now a second to the matter at hand
A trip to the Darkness below

"What have you done to me, you sick fuck?"
A smile. "Does it not satisfy?
An end to the pain that you felt was the deal.
In return are the souls you supply."
"The pain of my scars is drown out by far
By this hunger consuming my need.
I need to torment each one before death,
You bastard! Why do I only feed?"
"By feeding, my Slave, you harvest the souls
You promised me in our deal.
Never was torture a part of the bargain.
Go forth. There are more souls to steal."
"And once I have taken these souls you request,
Is that when you set me free?"
"As long as you live, someone will cause you pain.
You will always be Slave unto me."

Blazing insanity blooms in a rage
As hatred begins to stain
"The soul of anyone, then, can be taken
If they are causing me pain?"
A smile, formed of misunderstanding
Now spreads across the dark face
"That is the deal, my Slave. Just as long
As you bring the soul back to this place."
"But what of your soul, you ignorant fuck?"
The smile now beginning to fade.
"I bet devouring your soul voids it all . . .
This shitty deal I have made."
A pause, "Yes, Slave, my soul ends it all.
But freedom, you see, has its price.
You may be free of the deal we have made,
But you will never escape the device."

Locked in a gaze of thought and intent
The Slave and Thiever of Souls
Understanding, and the lack thereof
Threaten the grip of control
"To be a slave and be forced to feed,
Or feed after I've had my fun.
If those are the only two choices I have,
It's sure as hell not the first one."
The Thiever of Souls and the Slave then collide
With weapons of claw and of tooth
The Thiever now still, so quickly brought down
And the Slave, realizing the truth
As the soul of the Thiever and all those therein
Merge with the scars on his own
The voices now present inside his dark mind
Bring darker truths to be shown

"Slave, you have played the game out as we hoped,"
Sang the morbid chorus of loss.
"Each one of us were the victim before,
And won, to find losing the cost.
Would have been better to pull the damned trigger
Than take up the offer, you see.
No longer the Slave, but the Thiever of Souls.
Prisoner, you've set us all free.
Enjoy your new hell, and suffer for us,
As we will suffer no more.
But, just as promised, at least this new pain
Will drown out the scars of before.
Your life is now eternal death,
And eternally you will feed.
This is the price you're condemned to pay
For your selfish, vengeful greed."

**

Slow creeping castles in mind intertwine
With memories bled deeply with pain
Chaotic structure, foundations of fear
And lives of a dark crimson stain
Slivered intentions thrust deeply within
Black fingers which clutch death like gold
Breeding disfigured delusions of life
In a worm-ridden heart love can't hold
Distorted figures of flesh and of shadow
Vehemently spawning delusion
Embedded far within failure-worn skin
With morbid intent the intrusion
Tragedies breeding disease and a hunger
Consuming a weak self-control
Raging insanity, loss of humanity
Ravenous Thiever of Souls

Unspoken Token

Daniel Smith

In the distance, through the yonder
Comes the Circumstance of Chance
How he longs to find his other
As he stumbles through each dance
Incomplete and in disorder
Yet a smile so often shines
In the deepest of his tortures
Yet, each move becomes sublime
For even in the times
The stumble turns into a fall
He stands until he stumbles once again
As he dreams outside the lines
And finds the laughter in it all
Though sometimes not until the tears have shed

In the distance, through the yonder
One day there will come a glance
Someone stopping so to ponder
On such clumsy elegance
As her loneliness and torture
Start to fade for the first time
For she sees in such disorder
What's been missing all this time
A feeling so divine
And yet, so scary, will enthrall
As broken pieces start to fit again
The glance, returned in kind
As they both begin to fall
The unspoken token setting hearts to mend

In that moment, he'll discover
She's the partner in this dance

Long awaited, for no other
Ever gave him such a glance
And the distance will grow shorter
In between her heart and mine
Such elegant disorder
As our hearts become entwined
And after all the times
We felt alone throughout it all
We'll find that loneliness has met its end
Together, we will find
That we will rise within this fall
Until our hearts are soaring once again

Beware the Giant Midgets

Daniel Smith

If ever, oh ever, you happen to meet
A poor giant midget while out on the street
Pay him no mind but do not lower guard
For the lives of giant midgets are puzzling and hard
For trapped deep inside the six foot illusion
Hides three feet of anger, made worse by confusion
Struggling to figure out why so much space
Has been given to such a short, height-challenged race
To move among people, just trying to fit in
When on the inside they don't fit their own skin
The rage and the hatred they've let manifest
Into a mad need to put us to the test
To figure out why, when we fit our insides
There are places inside us where emptiness hides
Which we try to fill up with things we don't need
When all that they want is a chance to be freed
But if they could see that in fact we don't fit
Our minds contain people with nowhere to sit
Each with a voice that commands us to do
What it wants instead of what we want to do
Each one so loud as to drown out the rest
Each one insisting what it knows is best
Leaving us mostly distressed and confused
Our poor little brains worn out and abused
If they could just see that although they reside
Inside such a cavernous, double-sized hide
We are really no different than they
We all have our problems that won't go away
But they are alone, no one else in their mind
Festering within the shell they're confined
And we have the voices that tell us to guard
Against giant midgets, who have it so hard

Shadows Never Fade

Daniel Smith

High upon the valley
And low atop the hill
The shadows creep in darkness
As in light they never will
Dancing through the caverns
Or cavorting in the sky
Separated from their masters
As the darkness cuts their ties
Flying freely, sometimes gliding
Coinciding with the night
Never showing in their knowing
Of the coming of the light
Sweetly savoring each moment
Of the freedom they have won
'Til they're forced back into servitude
With the coming of the dawn

Hit Man's Lament
Daniel Smith

He sits on the shore of the River of Tears
Watching the world fail to improve
Thinking of all of the wasted years
Spent in suspension, waiting to move
Remembering ties to sanity's lies
And blood that so many times stained his hands
The smell of the screams and the taste of the cries
Unwanted rewards for filling demands
Each face of agony now an accuser
Pointing the finger of loss with a gaze
Each one a nail in the coffin of guilt
A dark silhouette in the lunatic haze
The voices inside compel him to move
Against humanity's tidal flow
Stilling the song of every heart
Placing them into the empty below
Then crying the tears of a prisoner's fears
Here in this unlocked cell of remorse
A sentence of draining and drowning in sins
As murderous silences all run their course
Nobody seeing the problems at hand
No one offering a hand of their own
Knowing that something is desperately wrong
Becoming a part of the problem unknown
And this lesser man, a rival to none
Knowing that things have gone way too far
Can muster up nothing but making the choice
Of letting these things remain as they are
For all of this pain was not his intention
And every effort a greater mistake
For ending all this would take much more life
Than the act of staying and suffering would take

It is hell, and such a deep hell
Knowing that every day is to kill
And nothing can break the cycle of tears
Nothing can stop the blood that is spilled
So he sits on the shore of the River of Tears
Watching the world fail to improve
Thinking of all of the wasted years
Spent in suspension, waiting to move

Already Gone

Daniel Smith

So long I've been struggling with myself
Can't find the words to make you understand my pain
The voices taking me belong to no one else
It eats away and it's driving me insane

I think I've lost my mind, and now I've lost my way
No matter how I try I can't make it go away
Is it such a crime to want to end this pain?
I wish that I could find some peace of mind before I die

Sleepless days, and nights that never end
A living hell inside the waking dream
Am I a zombie?
Am I the living dead?
When did laughter begin to drown the scream?

To think there was a time when I could stand and say
I'm happy just to be the man I am today
Somewhere down this line, my life began to fade
But you can't take a life that's already gone
I think I've lost my mind and now I've lost my way
No matter how I try I can't make it go away
Is it such a crime to want to end this pain?
I wish that I could find some peace of mind before I die

Set My Heart Free

Daniel Smith

I stare into your sightless scars as blood, like pain, comes raining down
And try to understand the reasons you have thrown yourself away
Mistakes befall us all, and you can't say that it was all your fault
Because a cruel bastard kept you subject unto fear and pain
And oh, I wish that I could take away from you those years and scars
And take upon myself the task of causing your tormentor pain
But some things just cannot be done when miles keep us separated
Words are all there are to offer and it's driving me insane
I turn my tear-streamed face into the maddened bliss of red descending
Letting crimson flows dissolve the salty stains of agony
Wishing I could find a way to say that you've been long deserving
So much more than you have come to let yourself believe
And there I see, above it all, a heart so full of grief and doubt
Consumed with so much hate for self, forgiveness cannot penetrate
Memories that every day betray and cast their chains of slavery
Keeping your heart prisoner, allowing thoughts to devastate
I reach out with my very soul, embracing your imprisoned heart
And summon all the love that one can possibly command
Concentrating every effort on the breaking of the chains
So you will not deceive yourself, and let yourself be damned
And oh, the woeful chorus of the angels who are now descending
Circling about you as I try to break the chains that bind
There I see the crimson rain is falling from the eyes of heaven
As the efforts of those very angels and my own combine
They sing of sweet forgiveness, and of letting go of pain unending
I wrap your heart more tightly in my love for you, both heart and soul
Angels whisper, "Oh dear heart, we're doing all that we can do.
It's up to you to break the chains and let your pain and self-hate go."
I shout above the choir, "Can't you see that you are loved?"
Praying you will understand that you have always had the key
Let it go, this pain and hate which you have fashioned as your cell
I can't lose you, my Angel. Can't you see you are the heart of me?

Truly Beautiful

Daniel Smith

Sometimes, it is the beauty we see in others
Despite them not seeing it for themselves
That shows us that, sometimes
What some may see as flawed or imperfect
Is nothing less than the rarest of beauty
So many fail to see it in themselves
That they begin to fail to see it on others, as well
For it gets harder to trust and to love
When so many only use their words as masks
Deceiving those who hold true to respect and honor
Until they fake their way in so as to take and abuse
And then tear them down
Oblivious to the pain they have inflicted
Sometimes proud of it
So many times causing such good hearted people
To believe it is they who have done something wrong
Until the loving person they were begins to fade
Retreating into a shell of depression, darkness, self loathing, and
hopelessness
Forgetting or denying how truly beautiful they are
And when someone finally sees in another
The same things they have failed to see in themselves
It opens their eyes
It awakens their soul
As hearts start to mend
Until there is beauty to be seen in the darkness again
Never gone, but merely overlooked and ignored
Once again shining forth in understanding
There is someone, just as they, who knows what it is to suffer
In every doubt, worry, and fear
In wounds self-inflicted or forced on by others
Whether physically or emotionally

And they begin to see the beauty on others, again, as well
In honor, truth, sincerity, and respect
Finally realizing for themselves much the same
Despite those who merely pretend so as to take and to harm
Until the darkness isn't so dark
Loneliness isn't so lonely
And even the worst of the pain can bring smiles
Shared between two perfectly imperfect souls
Who have found beauty in the world once again
By finding beauty in each other, and in themselves
When so many still refuse to see the same
Finding beauty in the darkness
Where once they could only find pain

Diary of the Damned – Tuesday, August 20th, 2013 – Second Entry

Daniel Smith

Intentions lay shattered and scattered about
Now remnants of what could not be
The veil rent asunder, revealing all doubt
And the face we tried hard not to see
The beautiful thistle amidst scores of thorns
Still pricks us, and begs us to bleed
Just as the dreams that we still so adore
Sometimes sprout from the darkest of seeds
When even hope falters, and faith seems a lie
When demons rejoice, and angels doth cry
And every step draws the conclusion much further away
Every tear that resides behind eyes
Far too weary to open upon their demise
Will still succumb to the fall despite their dismay
The death of mortality's endless charade
Lingers on as the lifeless continue to fade
Far beneath the parading of ghosts who continue to try
The cries of the broken a sweet serenade
Such an effortless potion that swiftly invades
The hearts of those who still refuse to die

The phantom progression of wanting the need
Still continues to tear at the soul
Ignoring the loss and the pain as it feeds
Upon every ounce of control
As the broken rise up from the fathomless ashes
Still screaming, and daring to dream
Holding to hope as it wails and it gnashes
Knowing nothing is all that it seems
While our time slips away with each grain through the glass
Our tears come and go, as the dew on the grass

And the frost of our frozen emotions still flees with the sun
We fall, and we rise, sprouting forth from the seeds
Of our failures and losses, and sweetly we bleed
Our journey through dark disenchantment now scarcely begun
Our every dream has been nearer than far
But none of us know just how close that we are
Until we dare to take just one step more
This thicket of briers now slowing us down
But protects the great beauty of what may be found
To be the very thing worth dying for

Forsaken Identity
Daniel Smith

Beyond the exoskeleton of labels and clichés
Resides a room without a door in the fabric of decay
Within the ragged corridors of self-loathing and fear
Where the person that we never want to be is drawing near
With every lie we tell ourselves and every step we fake
With every time we sell ourselves for less than what's at stake
Each time we find our future is the past we left behind
Each time we find a minute's peace has cost us peace of mind
The times the living disease becomes the disease of the living
The times we find that taking becomes easier than giving
When we find that serving self becomes the same as serving time
When we murder someone's trust and truly cannot see the crime
Each time we find our highs can be the lowest point of all
Each time we're not quite home without our backs against the wall
When smiling and laughter are the maddest times of all
When the calm before the storm becomes the walk before the crawl
The person that we never want to be begins to dwell
In the room without a door in our mental labyrinth cell
Dragging ragged fingernails across the coffin walls
Slowly breaking free from deep within the one who falls
The battle thus ensues between what is and what's to be
The tortured and the damned, both demanding to be free
Both manipulating and invading at each turn
Such hell as now both sanity and soul begin to burn
And from the silent corner, watching all without a word
Chaotically and sweetly biding time, there comes a third
Eagerly awaiting as each tears the other down
Clutching for the purchase which will cause the soul to drown
Dominating all the rotting conscious have become
The destroyer, come to permanently bleed out beyond numb
To the victor go the spoils of the spoiled, weary heart
In this dance of such a red, chaotic schizophrenic art

To honor, shame, or tragedy . . . where will your last breath lead
It all depends upon which dying fire you choose to feed

Carried Away
Daniel Smith

Holding on to everything
Crumbling to dust in my hands
There was never anything
That made me whole, and I understand
Although the things I've given
Have not been lost in vain
It was never meant for me
To live without this pain
Nothing that I've taken
Will I ever give away
These miseries I've stolen
Will go with me when I fade

My gifts aren't what I've given
But what I take away
I filled the emptiness inside
By drinking in your pain
Taking on your sorrow
Giving laughter in return
I've suffered under veils of smiles
And bled your tears in turn
I've saved you from these things that kill
I've sometimes left you numb
If nothing else, to save you
So that you will not succumb

This pain is like an anchor
It only pulls you down
And the undertow of agony
Will drag you from the shore
I couldn't say I love you
If I stood and watched you drown

Knowing I could save you
From the fate you had in store

Never think I hated you
For what I have confessed
I was always happiest
When I knew you suffered less
Know it was my choice
To draw your pain into my core
The only thing that pains me
Is I couldn't help you more
For my own private demons
They still scar me to this day
There was never anyone
To take my pain away
But I have learned to suffer
Finding heaven in this hell
Knowing I could keep you
From the darkness where I dwell

To be the one to sit inside
This unlocked cell of suffering
Choking on the ashes
Of memories that scream
Failing every day
To be the one who is recovering
From agonies I've stolen
So your sanity could breathe
Saving you has saved me
From the madness that entombs me
Helping me to battle
Through the darkest of my days
I just hope that when this life
Finally consumes me
That you'll be happy for me
As they carry me away

Cellar Door

Daniel Smith

Looking dead and empty from the outside
Every window dark and overgrown
A picture perfect not-so-sweet abandon
Standing long forgotten and alone
Beckoning to me with secret nothings
And stories each of us may never tell
A place that life and time have long forgotten
A place of death not far from living hell

Twisted vines tattoo the sides like cancer
Cataracts of dust enslave the glass
A jagged smile of railing slats now beckons
Waiting for the worst to come to pass
The steps, askew and incomplete, sustain me
As do the missing pieces of my mind
With every step, a creak that echoes louder
Than the silence that will fill the end of time

The door, now long ajar and slightly canted
Much like my eyes, half open to the truth
Sees through me, as I gaze into forever
Caressing every shadow of my youth
The surface, cracked and scarred like distant memories
Much like the hide of demons yet to be
Becomes as Braille beneath my trailing fingers
And whispers, "Come . . .," as fate opens to me

The corner shaves an arc on dusty floorboards
Motes now rise and sway, as if entranced
Every footfall landing past the threshold
Conjures more to join this ghostly dance
Etching upon stillness a reminder

That even the forgotten tend to change
Emphasizing time as an illusion
Every passing moment soon estranged

Traversing through each room, the memories linger
Linger but a moment do I dare
For in each dusty corner lies a shadow
Lying not, while hungry and aware
Every hallway stretches on eternal
No trace of salvation upon the stairs
Nothing here but promises now hollow
Forcing me out into fresher air

Wading through the overgrowth and briers
Working my way 'round this haggard shell
The cellar door awakens now from nowhere
Hinting both to heaven and to hell
Standing here in waiting, not in wonder
Not knowing how I know what soon will be
The cellar door extends its invitation
As it opens ever slowly unto me

Stepping into darkness disillusioned
Emptiness extends its open arms
Embracing me despite the separation
Beckoning me further in its charm
Crying, not in fear, but in elation
I stagger through my tears to my demise
The death of everything I had forsaken
Forgotten like the past I had disguised

In the furthest corner of my conscience
Crouching in the corner of the tomb
The child of devastation smiles sweetly
Driving every darkness from the gloom

Fighting not the chains that hold him captive
No longer forgotten and alone
For I have come to free him from the memories
And together, we will find our way back home

Living Death
Daniel Smith

Memories are made of scars
Woven into tapestries
Laid out in the darkest halls
Where schizophrenics roam
Voices sing of long-lost stars
Unique in their divinities
Written on the bathroom walls
Of rest stops long disowned
Twilight shines through broken panes
The hourglass remains the sane
Forever on its side
Though time goes creeping on and on
There are no truths within a name
With violence breeding out the same
Such darkness here resides
It must have been here all along
For the only lights remembered
Are the phantoms of dismay
The only satisfaction
Is it might not be a lie
The final dying embers
Are the fires that fuel decay
A comatose reaction
In a mind that never dies
Such dreams are never ending
Dying hearts cannot be stilled
The poison circulating
Now sustaining waking death
They rise in their descending
As in emptiness they're filled
More intoxicating
With their every failing breath

On legs that quake and tremble
Come euphoria and pain
Such sweet inoculation
In the cure that is disease
Their bodies now a temple
To the rotting and insane
The grave's ejaculation
To the soul upon its knees
Emptiness conscripted
On the question of forever
Eternity's dark sermon
In the Chapel of Decay
Such madness now inflicted
In the Valley of the Never
Consuming the uncertain
As the lifeless lead the way
These freely bleeding masses
To a pulse remain enslaved
Vainly grasping endlessly
For lives they'll never own
They sip from tainted glasses
On which failures are engraved
Harvesting so recklessly
The sorrows they disown
Finding false forgiveness
In their Mothers, Sons, and Gods
To ease their guilty consciences
So they can sin again
Blindly bearing witness
To their weakening façade
Giving darkness dominance
In times that soon will end
Forever so unknowing
That their lives are but pretend
So easily they free themselves

From any blame they earn
While every stone they're throwing
Will betray them in the end
They'll find that they themselves
All feed the fires in which they burn
While Death is biding time
From His throne He needn't move
With the blind leading the blind
In the place where liars rule
How they suffer so sublime
Each one trying so to prove
They the only King to find
In this bloody Land of Fools

Here's a sample from the follow-up publication:

Cry Love

Verse II: More New Voices

Poetry that grabs your heart…and squeezes

From Sarah Galo

A Final Scene in a Bar

The boundary of you and me, the boundary of us where you
and I could not and should not trespass
when his eyes measure your legs, the length around his waist,
your feet crossed at his hips
crossed over the line between us, when an embrace between
friends is no longer a simple goodbye
when he invites you to late night dinners, and even later night
walks in the park, or rather playground
chances to get metaphysical, an excuse to watch you as you
watch the stars...

From Ashley Rockhill

Broken Wings

I am not a phoenix
I descend
with wingless plummet
into madness.
Cradled by the glow of defeat
the roar of self-destruction
I burn.
Amongst the crackle
with acrid smoke
I embrace agony
with failure's devotion..